THE STEAM WORKSHOPS OF THE
GREAT WESTERN RAILWAY

THE STEAM WORKSHOPS OF THE
GREAT WESTERN RAILWAY

KEN GIBBS

The
History
Press

To all 'Craftsmen in Steam'.
In grateful memory of those past, in support of
those present, and with every good wish for those
yet to come (and come they will!)

Cover illustrations: Front: Work is underway in the lifting shop; Back: Stafford
Road Works under construction. (Both author's collection)

First published 2014

The History Press
The Mill, Brimscombe Port
Stroud, Gloucestershire, GL5 2QG
www.thehistorypress.co.uk

British Library Cataloguing in Publication Data.
A catalogue record for this book is available from the British Library.

ISBN 978 0 7509 5912 4

Typesetting and origination by The History Press
Printed in Great Britain

Contents

Acknowledgements

During my Great Western years, many friendships and contacts were made, and over the years some have fallen away whilst others have been maintained. This compilation of *Steam Workshops of the Great Western* has seen the reinforcement of old friendships and the renewal of some lost for a long period. New contacts have been made, and from many directions assistance has been afforded from old and new sources, with a notebook from here and a piece of paper from there, all coming together in this presentation of *Steam Workshops of the Great Western Railway*.

For omissions I can only apologise, but a great deal which has appeared, whether forms, photos or drawings, has sprung from many sources, and from odd items stored as souvenirs for many years by many people. Many now, like the author, are in their eighties! And some are no longer with us. Sincere thanks to all.

Ken Gibbs
LCGI (Mech. Eng.)
2014

Introduction

In my book *The Great Western Railway – How it Grew*, I introduced the reader to the constituent companies absorbed, developed, altered or put out of business by the expanding Great Western Railway (GWR). Included were details of the locomotive stocks affected by the takeover and the modifications using, where appropriate, standard Great Western fittings.

This book explains those notes with details of the locomotive maintenance and building facilities which came with, or were developed from or for the maintenance, building or rebuilding of those locomotives. The main GWR workshops at Swindon have been covered many times (but are included briefly here for continuity), whilst other facilities are rarely, if ever, mentioned in detail. It is intended that this book will fill a blank space in the current railway literature range, which already covers goods' sheds and goods' yards, along with running sheds, railway station architecture and civil engineering bridges, viaducts, etc.

Many of the buildings have now, taking Swindon as an example, been developed into shopping malls and commercial areas, or have disappeared in a cloud of demolition dust, as has Swindon's mighty 11.5-acre 'A' Shop steam locomotive repair and maintenance complex. One remaining original workshop (the old 'R' machine and fitting shop) now houses STEAM, the Museum of the Great Western Railway.

At other sites on the system, a number of the lesser workshops have survived, and have become part of the preserved/heritage railway scene, now in use for really far more than they were originally designed in the formative years, staffed usually by unpaid volunteers and railway enthusiasts.

These shops are often now accompanied by new or refurbished buildings housing the maintenance and rebuilding of the heritage carriage and wagon rolling stock, completing the total railway aspect.

At Swindon, this portion of the works was abandoned in 1964 and the maintenance of C & W stock combined and transferred to the locomotive workshops, now greatly reduced from the original layout, the whole ending in 1987 when the works closed. The remains are now a shopping mall and museum.

This book thus outlines the story and history of the founding, development, growth and eventual fate of the workshops associated with the development and demise of the GWR in its steam years.

Ken Gibbs

PART 1

1

Facilities for Maintenance and Construction

Thumbnail Sketches of Main Works and Facilities

From the early days, the proliferation of railways indicated very rapidly a missing ingredient in their make-up. Lines were laid to approved routes, locomotives and running stock obtained, finances (sometimes!) well organised, schedules for passenger and goods traffic arranged. And then arose 'maintenance'!

Having got the stock, the day-to-day running could be covered (the driver could always nip around with his long-spouted oil can!), but for deeper maintenance other facilities would be required. For the very heavy repairs there was always the manufacturer, but for general routine maintenance it seems the general philosophy was that if it was ignored, a problem would go away. Nothing really changes. Even today 'maintenance' is one of the least acceptable expenses.

In the early days, the problems were certainly worse, in that few could do the craft work, and often there was nowhere to actually work anyway. It was with some companies often with great reluctance that even the engine shed was built, let alone workshops, and there are on record several instances of locos being 'shedded' under bridges and station canopies. 'Maintenance' was pushed under the nearest stone in the hope that it would disappear, but of course it couldn't and wouldn't. It was an essential part of the railway system.

There is, of course, the now famous legend of both Brunel and Gooch working in the running shed at the London end of the Great Western line, in the attempt to improve the efficiency and reliability of the first locomotives. This introduces an additional requirement, coming under the heading of 'design' rather than repairs and maintenance, and particularly in the early years complicating the routine essentials. A component had to be made to work effectively, being altered if required, before its regular 'maintenance' could begin.

Even with the Great Western, taking the famous *North Star* as an example, the loco was delivered at Maidenhead in kit form several months before the 'running shed' was built, probably around it, in 1838. The loco had been temporarily stored, and we can visualise it sheeted down against the weather on a short length of track, as the connection from delivery barge to main line was not possible at that time. The main line had not reached the area.

At the London Paddington end, a two-part shed consisted of a 'stabling' end and a workshop end, in which heavier repairs and maintenance could be done, branching in two directions from a central octagonal 'roundhouse' with a turntable. Once again, the locos were available before the covered facilities, so that the first attempts at maintenance were done in the open air. An adjacent workshop facility was later built to enable the roundhouse building to be utilised wholly as a shed.

As the line progressed, so sheds, some temporary, were constructed to house the locomotive stock. In some instances, where there would not be the future requirement for a permanent running shed, a length of siding was constructed. One such siding (within a mile of where this book is currently being written), was at Hay Lane, just outside Swindon, the terminus of the Great Western line for about six months in 1840.

Hay Lane, just a spot on a country road between Swindon and Royal Wootton Bassett, actually had a canal wharf on the Wiltshire and Berkshire Canal en route through the valley below Swindon. This was probably the attraction as a ready-made supply point at the line's temporary end. Although still known as 'Hay Lane Wharf', it now takes an old Swindonian to point out the course of the long-gone canal, which is now part of a restoration programme.

There is no record of any form of running shed at Hay Lane, at this or any other period, but just back up the line the Great Western Workshops would be set out, with their own running shed, at roughly the topographical halfway point of the envisaged London–Bristol Railway. Brunel and Gooch were off the mark very quickly with regard to the building and maintenance potential for future Great Western steam. At Swindon, as at Paddington, it is more than likely that the shed and facilities were in use really before they finished construction, the finishing touches progressing around and above the locomotives.

The official opening date was 1 January 1843 for the Swindon Shed and Works, but the first shed of the system had been erected at Drayton in 1837. This was the first headquarters of Daniel Gooch when he commenced his quite awesome task with such confidence. About three months after his appointment he received the first two locomotives, albeit in 'kit' form, and erection under his supervision began. The locos were *Premier* and *Vulcan*, and both had been delivered by the opposition, the canal system, early in November from the makers, Messrs Tayleur of the Vulcan Factory, Lancashire. *Vulcan* was in steam before the year's end, although it was another four years before the dream of the London–Bristol line was actually fulfilled, and the line between the two cities opened.

The line actually joined Bristol to Bath as well; a connection opened in 1840 with its loco shed at the Bristol end. When the Bristol & Exeter Railway was finally amalgamated into the Great Western in 1876, the latter took over the B & E shed at Temple Meads and the locos were transferred there. The Great Western facilities in the early years around 1840 were known either as 'engine sheds', where a structure was actually built and was intended to be permanent, or as 'engine stations', where facilities for running and maintenance were to be available. In the latter case the facilities could be on a siding only with no cover, or with temporary cover until the line moved on toward completion.

As lines were added, and companies absorbed, so engine sheds and stabling points were allocated and constructed. The running shed became not only the stabling and routine servicing base, where coal and water stocks were maintained, but the obvious place where routine maintenance could be done – somewhere under cover where tools could be kept and maintenance staff based; where the locomotives could be worked on.

For major repairs recourse could be made to the manufacturers, but this was a far more difficult step than it appears on the surface. For small companies it must have been somewhat of a nightmare! Even for the Great Western it was, or would have been, difficult. The major problem of those formative years around 1840 would have been how to get the loco back at all. There was no direct connection to the manufacturer. The loco couldn't just be routed back over a railway network because there wasn't one. It would have to be returned the way it came, in kit form(!) and by water, with the canals playing a major part. Thus the development of a maintenance structure was really one of great importance, and one which led to the realisation that 'do it yourself' was the only practical way.

As construction of the railway progressed, and routine running commenced, a further requirement became obvious. Between major destinations, intermediate bases would need to be set up where not only could locomotives and stock be routinely serviced but where standby and replacement stock would need to be kept to cover breakdowns. Later, but sooner than was envisaged at the time, would come the further problem of dual track, and stock related to both broad- and standard-gauge rails, as the impact of the solely broad-gauge system faced. This was a problem confined really to the original Great Western Railway (GWR) and to broad-gauge constituents.

Thus arose the complication of broad- and narrow-gauge sheds at sites where the two met, as meet they would over the coming years, and the further problems of locomotives made by many and various manufacturers, all requiring spares and maintenance.

Mention has been made elsewhere of the vast difference between maintaining locomotives, and actually constructing locomotives. The notes that follow include thumbnail sketches of some of the facilities available to the railways, which were eventually absorbed by the Great Western, and which were big enough to support their own workshops where 'construction' was carried out as well as routine maintenance.

Whilst a number of such companies *built* some of their own locomotives, that does not signify that they actually *made* their own locomotives, in the way that 'making' at Swindon Works meant what it said. Foundry, rolling mill, heavy steam hammer and drop hammer facilities were not available at most sites to actually make the components that were used, particularly some of the larger items. For example, a cylinder block can be machined without being necessarily cast at the factory in question. So although some companies built their own locomotives, contractors had supplied some of the larger components in rough or 'finished' form.

There were of course those small companies that relied on other companies as manufacturers to supply stock on lease, often with a 'maintenance contract' as part of the deal. In this case, maintenance facilities in terms of buildings were virtually non-existent, as the small companies running very few engines over very short mileages could not afford such luxuries anyway. The reluctance to build even a running shed has been mentioned, so a works of any sort was out of the question. There are thus many companies absorbed by the GWR that had no facilities at all for repairing locomotives, except possibly a running shed of sorts with minimal hand tools and equipment.

Early shops had rope blocks and screw jacks for lifting, with no provision for overhead lifting. Often a portable 'shear legs' was available. These tripod structures are useful on occasions, and require considerable skill in use! Very large versions were in use generally in the early years of the railways; not confined to them of course – they were found in all sorts of civil and military applications, in the latter for mounting big guns or unloading transports. The three massive poles were lashed at the top and supported a naval-type block and tackle, which used ordinary hemp ropes and wooden pulley blocks.

Their use and requirement increased, and some very large examples finished as 'permanent' structures, erected and lashed in position adjacent to loco workshops. Eventually, the structures took a more standard form of large, bolted timber framings. Later, these gave way to iron, but in several instances a large wooden structure had been in use for years outside an early loco 'lifting' shop, or adjacent to the shed road, usually outside the shed allocated to 'casualties'.

With various 'lifting shops' dotted around on sites of absorbed companies, the need to standardise facilities was felt, and the Churchward era heralded the design and construction of a 'standard' lifting shop, either as new on a new site or as a replacement. Content included the usual hoist, ranging from 35- to 50-ton capacity, a smithing forge and equipment, and later on welding gear and related machine tools.

Lifting, always a problem with locomotive repairs, had to be dealt with safely. The open exposed nature of the ordinary shear legs developed into a wooden covered structure, e.g. the one erected at Bordesley shed about 1852. A later example from about 1908 (and 35 tons capacity as against 18 tons of the 1852 version) is actually inside a lifting shop (Oxley Sidings, Wolverhampton). Bordesley was replaced by the Tyseley Shops and Shed around 1908.

The following is an outline of some of the works of other companies which were big enough to have not only maintenance but also building facilities to construct, even from parts supplied by contractors, at least some of their own locomotive stock. The closure or retention of such facilities occurred when the company concerned fell within the Great Western's expansion net!

Preamble

Swindon Works, which dominated the Great Western for the first half of the twentieth century, was really only one facet (true, a major facet) of the Great Western diamond. Before Swindon Works existed, experienced contractors were making locomotives for the developing world systems, as well as for the embryonic Great Western Railway (GWR).

At the end of Great Western steam there were on the system a number of major works, divisional works and the smaller 'lifting shops' where steam repairs were undertaken, sites which had been acquired or had become a necessity brought about by the inexorable expansion of the Great Western from its small broad-gauge beginnings (see my book *The Great Western Railway – How it Grew*).

Swindon Works suffered a double blow with the end of steam. At about the same time came the end of the Carriage and Wagon Works, virtually half of the works site, which shut down completely. This was followed by the progressive diminution of work at the locomotive half remaining. Carriage and wagon work, such as it was, was crammed into the remaining ex-steam locomotive shops.

Little new was made, and less and less was repaired, in the now much reduced works as the years passed. Twenty years after the end of steam, the works itself had closed and demolition begun. The works had struggled against the odds, some of its own making, during this last period. A shopping and industrial complex now spans much of the old site, a sad end to one of the world's best-known locomotive and carriage works.

With the end of steam the same fate had overtaken the divisional repair shops and the smaller lifting shops spread over the system, each of the latter attached to a better-known running shed, the haunts, both officially and unofficially of keen schoolboy (and other) number takers. Most of the shops which formerly undertook those steam repairs that did not require a major job at a main works departed from use and some from very existence during the 1960s. (Some were converted for diesel use, which amounts to the same thing!)

The works owned and operated by the Great Western were not the only ones to suffer the demise of steam. The manufacturers of contract orders also suffered. Those which had not diversified before the virtually predictable premature end of the steam locomotive faced severe problems. Well-known names had merged and amalgamated years before in the attempt to stay in business, but a number could not compete in the new diesel and electric field and, as with the railway companies' steam workshops, were forced to close.

However, during the preceding twenty years Great Western design had petered out to be superseded by a new era of steam construction. The new 'standard' steam locomotives, looking nothing like their Great Western forbears, were really hybrids spawned by nationalisation of the railway system and were themselves to be short-lived. They were to be the ultimate in steam locomotive design – designs still really being developed – but steam was cut off in mid flow and virtually new engines were consigned to the scrap merchants' oxytorch. Live steam had disappeared!

Some of these locomotives, very few and themselves often partially demolished, after rusting quietly away for several years, suddenly became very desirable items for cannibalising and rebuilding by dedicated enthusiasts at a number of small, privately owned railway projects. Some of the accompanying buildings at the various sites had also survived or were rebuilt from dereliction. The humble lifting shop had returned, in a number of instances, not to its original use but to far more than that, in some cases augmented or expanded by further structures.

The facilities of major works used for steam repairs, have generally long since vanished, and the locomotives themselves are being returned to service from a condition of disrepair completely unheard of when they were running in their steaming days. Some small lifting shops and ex-running sheds, often partially rebuilt, far from being 'maintenance' bases, have now become the main works, limited equipment notwithstanding. With enthusiasm and ingenuity playing a major role in loco repair, both amateur and professional (often retired) craftsmen are now involved in steam repairs and rebuilding.

The purpose of this book is thus to give a general outline of the usually obscured or hidden facets of the development and growth of the GWR workshops with some emphasis on the hows and whys of the maintenance and manufacture of its steam locomotive stock. (The effect the railway had on its opposition, the canals and other railway companies, is discussed in my book *The Great Western Railway – How it Grew*.) This book details the where, how, why and by whom the locomotives were designed, made and maintained.

Great Western steam still exists. It is hoped permanently.

Construction, Repair and Maintenance Facilities: Great Western Railway

MAJOR WORKS

SWINDON	1846–1987	
WOLVERHAMPTON (Stafford Road)	1860 expanded 1932	closed 1964
CAERPHILLY	Expanded 1925	closed 1966
NEWTON ABBOT	1893	closed 1962
WORCESTER	1852–1889	closed 1965
OSWESTRY	1860	closed 1965
BARRY	1893	closed 1964
SHREWSBURY	1856	closed 1967

DIVISIONAL WORKS

Division	Built	Repair Depot
BRISTOL	1935	BRISTOL BATH ROAD
CARDIFF VALLEYS (Taff Vale Railway) Repair Shop	1884–1929	BARRY & CATHAYS 5-ROADS
LONDON	1838–1854	PADDINGTON
LONDON	1906	OLD OAK COMMON
NEATH	1907	CARMARTHEN & DANYGRAIG
NEWPORT (Maesglas)	1915	NEWPORT EBBW JUNCTION
NEWTON ABBOT	1893	NEWTON ABBOT (workshops of the old South Devon Railway)
OSWESTRY		OSWESTRY (workshops of the old Cambrian Railway)
WOLVERHAMPTON	1908	(like Old Oak) TYSELY (replaced smaller depot at Bordesley)
WORCESTER	1852	WORCESTER (workshops of the Oxford, Worcester & Wolverhampton Railway)

REPAIR & LIFTING SHOPS – CHURCHWARD STANDARD

		BUILT
ABARDARE	2 Roads	1909
EBBW JUNCTN (Maesglas)	Traverser	1915 (Division works)
LLANELLY	2 Roads (1 outside)	1925
ST PHILLIPS MARSH BRISTOL	2 Roads	1910 (extended later)
STOURBRIDGE	1 Road	1926
TYSELY	Traverser	1908 (Division works)
OLD OAK COMMON	Traverser	1906 (Division works)
OXLEY	2 Roads	1907 (35-ton hoist)
CHELTENHAM	2 Roads	1907
PENZANCE	1 Road	1914
WESTBURY	1 Road	1915
BRISTOL BATH ROAD	2 Roads	1935
CARDIFF EAST DOCK	1 Road	1931
DIDCOT	1 Road	1932
LANDORE	1 Road	1932
STAFFORD ROAD LIFTING SHOP	1 Road	1860 (?) (rebuilt 1931)
BANBURY	1 Road	1944
SOUTHWALL	1 Road	1883 (rebuilt 1954)
READING	1 Road	1932

OXFORD	1 Road	c. 1900 (extended 1931 with heavier hoist)
YEOVIL	1 Road	1857
WEYMOUTH	1 Road	1885 (in 1930 35-ton replaced 20-ton crane)
TAUNTON	1 Road	1932
EXETER	1 Road	1894
TRURO	1 Road	1900
CROES NEWYDD	1 Road from table	1902
GLOUCESTER	1 Road wheel drop	1872
LYDNEY	1 Road	1868
HEREFORD	4 Roads	1853
CARDIFF CANTON	1 Road	1882 (1925 new Shop + Hot Wash Plant
SEVERN TUNNEL JUNCTION	1 Road	1908 (Repair Shop c. 1938)
DUFFRYN YARD	1 Road	1896 (Repair Shop extended 1931)
DANYGRAIG	1 Road	1896
CARDIFF (EAST DOCK)	1 Road	1931
WESTBOURNE PARK LS	1 Road	1898 (closed 1906, 91 × 23ft 6in)
WESTBOURNE PARK REPAIR SHOP	4 Roads	1855 (extended 1882, closed 1906)
ABERYSTWYTH	At end of 2-Road shed	Enlarged 1936
TONDU	2 extended Roads	1889 (used for repairs)
LAIRA (PLYMOUTH)	1 Road smithy only	1901

All the above shops closed to steam during the 1960s and some were converted or adapted for diesel traction support.

Facilities in lifting shops included 35-ton hoists and, in divisional and two-road shops 30- or 35-ton overhead cranes. Those constructed after 1930 had 50-ton hoists.

Divisional shops had twelve pits, each 52ft long.

Two-road shops had pits 95ft long.

One-road shops had pits 68ft long.

SOME EARLY WORKS OF COMPANIES ABSORBED OR REPAIR SHOPS OF GWR 'NON STANDARD'

BIRKENHEAD	Repair Shop. 2 Roads. Birkenhead Railway Works. Opened 1840. Closed 1878. To GWR & LNWR 1860.
BORDESLEY JUNCTION	Smithy only. Opened1855. Closed 1908.
BRISTOL TEMPLE MEADS	Old Bristol & Exeter Works. Opened 1850. Closed 1934.

CARDIFF (EAST MOORS)	Shed closed in 1926 then used as workshop.
CARDIFF DOCKS (Ex Rhymney Railway)	Loco shop 165 × 50ft. Carriage shops 180 × 50ft. Running repairs only from 1901. Heavy repairs to Caerphilly.
CARNE BRAE (Hayle Railway)	Opened 1838. Main depot and workshops. Repair shop for the west until Truro was rebuilt in 1900. Taken over by Cornwall Railways 1846, GWR 1876. Altered 1879. Small smithy built 1896. Closed 1917.
CIRENCESTER	Workshops of the Midland South Western Junction Railway. opened 1895. Closed 1924.
DANYGRAIG (Rhonda & Swansea Bay)	Workshops loco and carriage.
FALMOUTH (Cornwall Railway)	Opened 1863. Fitting shop, about 18ft × 16ft. Removed 1897.
LLANELLY DOCK	Fitting shop. Opened 1840. Closed 1925.
MERTHYR	Fitting shop. Opened 1841. Closed 1846.
NEATH (Neath & Brecon Railway)	Fitters shop. Opened 1864. Closed 1946.
NEWPORT (Bolt Street)	Erecting shop. Monmouthshire Railway. Opened 1854. Closed 1918 and demolished. Two 7-bay roads with centre deep pit traverser.
OXFORD	Fitting shop. Opened 1850. Closed 1876. (Oxford, Worcester & Wolverhampton Railway)
PADDINGTON (GW)	Repair bays to east side of roundhouse. Opened 1838. Closed 1858.
PENARTH DOCK	Shed with machine shop and smithy. Opened 1887. Closed 1929. (Taff Vale Railway)
PENZANCE	Small fitting shop. West Cornwall Railway. Opened 1852. Closed 1876. Rebuilt 1876. Closed 1914.
PLYMOUTH (MILLBAY)	South Devon Railway. Opened 1849. Closed 1924. (Temporarily opened until 1931) Carpenters' shop and smithy. Lifting shop added in 1884.
PORTHMADOG	The Boston Lodge Workshops of the Ffestiniog Railway. 2ft gauge. Opened 1836 and still open after closing in 1937. Second World War stripped for salvage reuse. Resurrected 1996 and expanded into Welsh Highland Railway. Surrounded by but not part of GWR. The line itself is a tourist attraction with mostly volunteer staff.
READING	On main Paddington–Bristol line. Engine shed. Opened 1840. Closed 1880. Rebuilt 1880 Bristol side of station with roundhouse shed and 90ft × 30ft single-road lifting shop incorporated. Completely redesigned and rebuilt in 1930–32 with a straight road shed and a separate 84ft × 42ft lifting shop.
STOURBRIDGE JUNCTION	Fitting shop. Opened 1870. Closed 1926. Reopened 1944. Closed c. 1965 at end of steam.
SWANSEA DOCKS	Westlake (contractors) engine shed and works. Opened 1894. Closed 1898.

ST BLAZEY	Repair shops and HQ of the Cornwall Mineral Railway.
TALLYLYN JUNCTION	Brecon & Merthyr. Originally a running shed. Opened 1863. Converted 1869 to engine and wagon shops. By 1903 a carriage shed.
MACHAN	Brecon & Merthyr Workshops; could also have been the workshops of the earlier Rumney Railway.
TAUNTON	Bristol & Exeter Railway. Open 1842. Smithy closed 1860.
TAVISTOCK	South Devon & Tavistock Railway. Opened 1859. Closed 1865. GW taken over in 1876. Very small fitting shop.
TENBY	2-Road fitting shop opened 1863. Closed 1932. 105ft × 28ft and 64ft × 15ft. 1907 loco repairs transferred to Carmarthen.
TONDU HP	Llynvi & Ogmore Railway. Workshops with loco shed.
TROWBRIDGE	Smithy and a separate fitting shop. 15ft × 15ft at the end of the shed (3-line).
WESTBOURNE PARK	About 1872 workshops and repair shop (single line). Repair shop enlarged late 1880s and a lifting shop built 1898. Depot closed and replaced by Old Oak Common 1906 (opened 1855).

FACILITIES FOR MAINTENANCE AND CONSTRUCTION

Railway workshops used for locomotive construction and subsequently absorbed by the Great Western:

Swindon Works

Wolverhampton Works

The Taff Vale Workshops, West Yard, Cardiff Docks

The Bristol & Exeter Workshops, Bristol

Monmouthshire Railway & Canal Co., Newport, Bolt Street Works

Cambrian Railway Works, Oswestry

Caerphilly Works, Rhymney Railway

Newton Abbot Works, South Devon Railway

Worcester Works, Oxford, Worcester & Wolverhampton Railway

Carn Brea, West Cornwall Railway

LOCOMOTIVE BUILDERS & REPAIRERS ASSOCIATED WITH THE GWR AND ITS CONSTITUENT COMPANIES

Bury – early obsession with 0-4-0 locos. First locos for London & Birmingham Railway 1846

Foster & Rastrick – Stourbridge – Agenoria Science Museum. Shutt End Railway Kingswinford to Staffordshire & Worcestershire Canal

Hazeldines Foundry near Bridgenorth – build loco for Trevethick in 1808

Beyer, Peacock & Co. – for GWR 1855 & MSWJ Railway 1898

Sharp, Steward – Tank loco. Brecon & Merthyr Railway 1865

Slothert & Slaughter – 1821–1888–1935 Monmouthshire Railway

E.B. Wilson – for Oxford, Worcester & Wolverhampton Railway 1854

Messrs Kitson Co. – built *Ely* 1851 for Taff Vale to Taff Vale designs

Rothwell & Co. – Goods locos 1841 and for Bristol & Exeter 1853 (Pearson's design)

E B Wilson & Co. – built the Jenny Bird Class for OW&W Railway

William Fairbairn & Son – built and for West Midland Railway 1860s

Beyers – Manchester

Robert Stephenson & Co.

Vulcan Foundry

Low Moor Ironworks

Sharp Stewart & Co. – 1890

Manning Wardle

George England

Hosgood – Barry Railway

Gruning Company

Stewarts

Hunslet Engine Co.

Chapman & Furneauz

Jones

Davies & Metcalfe

Dübs

Tyrell

Kitson Naismith

Yorkshire Engine Co.

Peckett & Co.

Timothy Hackworth – Shildon

Johnson & Kinder – Wolverhampton Repairers

Horsely Ironworks for the St Helen's Railway

Parfitt & Jenkins – 1872–75 (Alexandra Docks)

Bagnall – (Narrow 1ft 11¼in gauge – Vale of Rheidol)

Cooke Loco Co. – New Jersey, USA – 1899

Hurry Riches – Rhymney Railway

Nasmyth Wilson – later Nasmyth Gaskell

Hudswell Clarke – Port Talbot Railway 1900

Worcester Engine Co. – Alexandra Docks 1868

R & W Hawthorn – Alexandra Docks 1884

Fletcher Jennings – Severn & Wye Railway 1873

Andrew Barkley – Llanelly & Mynydd Mawr Railway 1907

Fox Walker – Llanelly & Mynydd Mawr Railway 1875

Brush Electrical – Powlesland & Mason Railway 1903–06

Avonside Works – Bristol 1862

George England & Co. – *c.* 1863

PART 2

1

The Developing Influence of the GWR and its Two Main Workshops at Swindon and Stafford Road, Wolverhampton

The Great Exhibition held in London 1851 had shown to the world of that period some of the technological achievements possible. The slow-moving progress of the preceding centuries had suddenly begun to accelerate with ingenious and far-reaching developments in a number of fields, none more so than in iron and steel and related products. The whole was epitomised in railway terms by the display of the Great Western's 8ft broad-gauge single *Lord of the Isles*.

Thomas Carlyle has recorded that the greatest influence on mankind has been gunpowder, printing and the Protestant religion, which, whilst at the period playing a major role in the life of Britain, with the latter firmly established and the two former caught up in the technological advances being made, the addition of the combination of steam with iron and steel developments very rapidly changed the world's face and the outlook of its peoples. This progress in communication was of necessity rapid in Europe and the USA and much slower in reaching other countries to which technological advances now completed could be transplanted when opportunity arose.

The work of Bolton, Watt, Newcomen and the like had progressed from an earlier age and related technology, from the eighteenth century to the mid-nineteenth century, through the period of Trevithick, and of Murray and Blenkinsop, Hedley and Hackworth, Braithwaite and Ericsson, and to the years of the Victorians, who revelled in the progress and the entrepreneurial, wide-thinking technological age it had heralded.

As the waterwheel had been applied to replace man and the horse, so steam had, in many applications, replaced the waterwheel. Wherever coal, charcoal and wood could be obtained or transported, so steam power could replace other traditional methods of obtaining power.

Embryo industries had already slowly spread, in ribbons of development, along the banks of sluggish water contained in the network of canals that traversed the land in an increasing web, ribbons which had expanded over the last fifty or so years, and around which at various points prosperous towns had developed.

Transport of essentials right to the very doorsteps of use was possible, with particular emphasis on the movement of coal, the steam producing essential. Canals were the links between rivers, themselves always a potential for transport, and the network of waterways transported people and products across the land in a slow but positive communication system with the potential of the interlinking plateways and tramroad soon to be exploited.

Steam had to a considerable extent reduced the use of the waterwheel as a power source from the 1700s, progressively over the following years introducing power to places where no rivers flowed and no waterwheel could function. The beginnings of industrial might need no longer be located on the banks of flowing water, all competing for the power dictated by the vagaries of weather and rainfall and season.

When Brunel and Gooch had examined their rail system for a suitable site for a repair depot, criteria had included availability of land and its position, which needed to be roughly midway between the major cities of London and Bristol.

Standing in the green fields of the Vale of White Horse, the pair couldn't fail to be aware not only of the iron tracks of the Cheltenham & Great Western Union Railway, which were en route to join their own just to the east of the selected site, but also of the silver ribbons of water which emphasised the closeness of their competitors to their own gleaming lines of rail, disappearing in the distance to London in the east and to Bristol, eventually, in the west, although currently terminating at Hay Lane, a mile or so from Swindon to the west.

The Wiltshire & Berkshire Canal dated from the mid 1790s and also roughly traversed east to south-west through the vale, whilst, snaking from a junction and heading north, the North Wilts Canal formed a transport link in use since 1819, to the Thames & Severn Canal, out of sight further north. The southern end of the Wilts & Berks was linked to the Kennet and Avon at Semington and its eastern end joined the Thames at Abingdon.

The winding narrow way of the Wilts & Berks had for fifty years quietly carried coals in and agricultural produce out of the vale, its only rivals the packhorse, the haulier and the mail coach over roads of uncertain reliability, also dependent on weather, rainfall and season.

General progress of industrial expansion continued; smoke from chimney stacks springing up from this expansion was becoming visible from all points of the compass as the developing power of steam was accepted.

The chimney stacks had already spread, by 1851, to the green Vale of White Horse in Wiltshire. Several miles away from the little agricultural town-on-the-hill of Swindon, indeed the tops of the stacks were well below the level of the scattered houses, a rectangle of very new buildings surrounded by green fields was becoming the nucleus of an establishment where steel, iron and steam were being combined in a quite outstanding way. Swindon Railway Works was on the map and functioning.

Building at Swindon was not of course unique. The railway builders were at work all over the country, the spread of the chimney stacks being either preceded, accompanied or followed by the ribbons of railway line snaking out on the ground, almost as fast as the smoke from the stacks spread above. The opening in 1825 of the Stockton & Darlington Railway had been the starter's gun, and the race was on.

Railway proposals were mooted, the cash raised by entrepreneurs and speculators, and railways commenced in the most likely and, it must be said, unlikely places imaginable. Fortunes were made rapidly and just as rapidly lost as schemes collapsed, leaving unpaid men and bills, and partly completed rail systems stopped at the first major problem.

The fever heat of speculation in the 1830s and '40s and an obsession with the advances of science and technology meant that money from the inexperienced was poured into schemes proposed by the inexperienced, to be operated by the inexperienced who, unless they possessed exceptional qualities, were stumped by the first problem that arose and to which they had no answer – in fact, a repeat of the canal boom of fifty years previously.

Bankruptcies, closures, takeovers, amalgamations are by no means a twentieth-century phenomenon. Many of the early railways floundered because of inadequate planning, hurried presentation of incomplete Bills through Parliament, long drawn out land acquisition and access problems, lack of sufficient funds and capital, useless management and operating staff; the list contains all the ingredients of failure in any combination chosen. Even when running there were cases of so-called dividends paid to shareholders from capital! Such was the railway 'boom'.

Of those that survived combinations and amalgamations were often the result of competition, found to be costly, and the principle that the bigger you are the less chance of failure there is. If failure does come, it is just that much bigger.

Many of the early companies then being involved with railways, a new phenomenon, were often extremely small, just made for joining two or three points of commercial interest and often backed by other railway companies. The sometimes urgent requirement for maintenance facilities became rapidly apparent, the actual builders of the rolling stock at first being the only contract source of repairs available to the newly formed companies.

Some contractors themselves in the early years were almost as inexperienced as the railway companies and certainly on occasions turned out some unreliable rolling stock of questionable design and material, as well as the use of questionable manufacturing techniques. When problems arose with the stock, or repairs were required, items and spares were found to be non-existent as the companies themselves had either a 'one-off'-style order book or had gone out of business. It was then up to the purchaser to do what he could.

In most cases there was little 'standardisation', and even components from locomotives of the same design were not interchangeable. Another obvious example of non-standardisation was that of the for-and-against arguments regarding width between the wheels or the 'gauge' controversy – 7ft 0in or 4ft 8½in – or some other size? Which should it be?

The persuasive far-sightedness of Brunel had proved an irresistible spur to adoption of the wide or broad gauge by the instigators of the Great Western Railway, initially in isolation, and for a time general pressure for broad gauge succeeded and the mileage of 7ft 0in increased, but from early success, however, it was slowly bottled up and contained.

At this period 7ft 0in and 4ft 8½in were not the only measurements considered. The Blackwall and Eastern counties area had 5ft 0in chosen by their Mr Braithwaite – 5ft 6in was attempted by one of the Scottish railways. It had to be Ireland which came up with the funniest attempt of the lot however. Half the line of the Belfast to Dublin, by the Ulster Railway Company, was being laid to 6ft 2in gauge, quite a reasonable decision for the 25 miles of track. The other half of the line, by the Drogheda Company, setting out from Dublin to meet up with the Ulster section, adopted a gauge a foot narrower at 5ft 2in.

The Directors of the Ulster line, immediately on becoming aware of the discrepancy, complained to the Irish Board of Works. The answer was a real classic and the story itself is recorded in a book of 1884. The board acknowledged the differences, but dismissed them by saying that although the lines were well under way at both extremities there was so little chance of them ever meeting in the middle that it wouldn't really matter anyway! A compromise was struck. The Irish tracks were to be 5ft 3in apart and at that decision progress in Ireland continued.

Although eventually adopted in America as standard, 4ft 8½in was not used in some other countries abroad, and various gauges for 'full size' – as opposed to 'narrow-gauge' specials – ranged from 3ft 6in to 5ft 6in throughout the empire, as it then stood, and other independent countries made their own choice.

The subject of gauges was also of general interest to the public and a letter in a magazine of 1867 emphasised that interest, and also recorded the gauges in use throughout a number of world countries. It seems that, although Britain was the first, no one was able to agree on the 'best' track gauge, and there was only an attempt at standardisation in some of the countries, including Britain, which had several different measurements.

There were very powerful arguments against not only the 7ft 0in but also against the 4ft 8½in. Contenders claimed that whilst the 7ft 0in gauge was obviously too wide the 4ft 8½in was just as obviously too narrow and a width of 5ft 3in or 5ft 6in should be adopted. Such was the dominance of objection to the 7ft 0in gauge in the arguments that the 4ft 8½in objectors were ignored as long as the strength of objections against 7ft 0in continued. By the time calmness returned 4ft 8½in had spread virtually everywhere, whilst pressure to spread the broad gauge continued from the Great Western sphere with diminishing success, being finally contained and stopped.

Starting as a completely broad-gauge line, with the new works at Swindon expanding for purely broad-gauge stock, the Great Western pushed on from London to Bristol and over tracks eventually to Penzance; then from Swindon through Gloucester to South Wales and to Milford Haven and through Oxford to the north as far as Wolverhampton. Other companies were also adopting the broad gauge in the first flush of enthusiasm.

Whilst the broad-gauge locomotives of Gooch went from strength to strength, the broad gauge itself started to decline in popularity and general adaption. The added requirements of size and that associated 'loading gauge', which ensured clearances at bridges, stations, tunnels and so on, meant that everything was to be built on the grand scale. Stability, speed and comfort were unquestionably the best anywhere, but costs, then as now, proved a factor in the whole question of viability and standardisation of gauge.

To the north, in the Wolverhampton area, the broad gauge ground to a halt and transfers of goods and passengers to the now accepted narrow-gauge lines of 4ft 8½in became necessary. Why 4ft 8½in no one knows; it was merely a 'traditional' figure which continued in use from tramways and had been earlier used by the Stephensons.

Maintenance then was a complicated affair, with all sorts of designs and early standards as such prevailing. An example of such a problem was that experienced by Swindon Works during 1855. When narrow-gauge locomotives were designed and built by Gooch for use at Wolverhampton, where 'mixed-gauge' lines existed, that batch of twelve had to be transported north on special wagons as they did not fit the track to enable them to steam to their destination.

When Brunel, with Gooch, had agreed that the valley overlooked by Swindon would be suitable for the site of his railway workshops, Brunel had already experienced some of the problems the railway builders suffered. Early locomotive designs by contractors were often not suitable, nor were they as reliable as they should have been, partly due, it must be said, to certain design criteria laid down by Brunel. The only alternative was, as is often the case, 'If you want a job done well, do it yourself!', but Brunel, brilliant engineer though he was, was not an experienced locomotive engineer. He needed some assistance.

Daniel Gooch, at the age of 20, following the now classic letter of application to Brunel, had become the locomotive man of the Great Western, later bringing as his assistant Archie Sturrock from Dundee. By the 1850s production was well under way at Swindon with a good measure of standardisation already to the fore within the broad-gauge sphere.

In the rest of the country the lines were spreading rapidly outside the sphere of influence of the Great Western; other companies were also becoming powerful in their own right and the spread of 4ft 8½in rails was rapidly becoming the accepted standard.

Great difficulties were being experienced in the search for, and spread of, supporters of the broad-gauge system and by about 1860 the broad gauge could be seen to be obsolescent.

The difficulties had led inevitably to a 'split' system. To the north the 4ft 8½in gauge was the main contender, with the recently acquired Stafford Road Works at Wolverhampton dealing with stock repairs covering the area Birkenhead, Worcester, Chester, Shrewsbury, Newport and Oxford to London. The broad gauge still thrived in the south, with its stock maintained at Swindon, and covered the area to the west, from London through Swindon, Gloucester, Cardiff and Milford, Bristol and Weymouth, and eventually down into Cornwall.

In the eastern half of the area the insidious and unstoppable spread of the narrow gauge had covered, or been inserted into, the broad-gauge system to reach its tentacles to Oxford,

Didcot, Basingstoke and London, eventually spreading in 1872 to Swindon in combination with a third-rail addition to the broad-gauge track.

The operation of installing the third rail makes interesting reading and an observer of the procedure between Hereford and Gloucester in 1869 recorded the following insight. As part had already been completed from Gloucester to Grange Court the line closed for two weeks between Hereford and Grange Court and passengers transferred by road around the closure.

A gang of 450 men from the area, who regularly worked on the Hereford Division, were selected and were to lodge during the completion of the work in a broad-gauge 'train of covered wagons, carefully whitewashed, and supplied with an abundance of clean straw and new sacks, the staff occupying a first class carriage for the night'. On Sunday at 4 a.m. the sleeping train moved along the selected track on which an engineer had marked by flags the work length for one ganger and twenty-two men. The 450 operators so distributed, the work was completed in five days and the line reopened on Friday. Another 22 miles of mixed track had been added to the system.

The fixation by the gauge war protagonists on the width of the track gauge obscured the potential of the assets of the broad-gauge system and the Great Western was inevitably the loser.

The spread of narrow-gauge lines generally and the need to construct ever increasing numbers of new locomotives, whilst also carrying the commitment to maintain and repair existing stock, meant a gross overloading of the northern section narrow-gauge workshops at Stafford Road.

The shops had been built in 1849 by the Shrewsbury & Birmingham Railway, a narrow-gauge organisation to be joined by the Great Western's broad gauge five years later. Later on we mention how fate plays tricks with careers when takeovers occur (an example being G.J. Churchward and Newton Abbot Works) and here the fates also took a hand. Joseph Armstrong was tucked away in the Saltney Works of the Shrewsbury & Chester Railway, itself taken over with the Shrewsbury & Birmingham by the Great Western in 1854.

There was now a mixed-gauge requirement for the area and a reorganisation was needed. The Stafford Road Works was selected as the main base of operations, and the Armstrong association with the Great Western had begun; a man in the right place at the right time. The small Shrewsbury & Birmingham Works was not really adequate for the increased requirements of centralising responsibilities, and plans were drawn up for expansion to include building of new stock – already well established – in broad-gauge terms at Swindon. Whilst expansion as such was to prove difficult, a major rehash of facilities was certainly possible and was completed by 1859. The old goods yard now sported a new foundry and boiler shop and the old running shed and repair shops had become the erecting and machine/fitting shops respectively; two lengths of pit were retained in the shed site for locomotive erecting.

Developments continued. The Great Western acquisition of the Birkenhead Railway in 1860 was followed three years later by the takeover of the West Midland, adding 21 and 131 locomotives respectively to the stock to be maintained. Stafford Road Works had to expand again and this time the move was across the main road where the broad-gauge sheds were located. Next to them were built another erecting shop accompanied by the usual smithy, fitting and machining facilities. The erecting shop was of the pits and traversing table design as at Swindon, although many railways preferred the long pit, end-to-end-type shop, which, whilst making internal movements more difficult, saved on the space taken by the table. And so the works remained for a number of years, split by a road and hemmed in by other developments.

The northern section, as regards maintenance, was separated into north 'northern' and north 'southern' areas, the latter being formed in 1889 as the Worcester Division to remove the pressures from Stafford Road Works.

In 1866 a broad-gauge order on Swindon signalled the end of the broad gauge, with the building of half a dozen side tank 0-6-0s with condensing arrangements for the exhaust steam from the cylinders to allow usage over the Metropolitan lines of the early London underground. These 'Sir Watkins' were the last broad-gauge engines constructed but repair and rebuilding of the other classic designs over the years made certain that broad gauge continued until the fateful date in 1892, at this time nearly thirty years in the future, when the end would come.

By about 1875 narrow-gauge track had, along with its relevant stock, all but ousted the wide gauge, which still with dignity and comfort hurried along its remaining course from Paddington to Penzance. The original concept of Brunel and Gooch had now returned almost to its starting point of 1841 with regard to track coverage.

Swindon at this time had been forced to take not just the odd order for narrow-gauge stock to help out but to actually consider that its future lay in adapting to the now standard gauge in all things. The importance of Swindon Works had not manifested itself into the general pattern of things locomotive as yet; its fame was still to come.

Rebuilding of locomotives at Wolverhampton accelerated in what could be called an experimental phase. Various engines from the West Midland Railway, taken over as runners, were examined and altered at Wolverhampton, as was a batch of Swindon-built 2-4-0s. Some West Midland Railway stock remained unaltered, one batch continuing in its original area of work and stabling, but some contract locos by Beyer were rebuilt from tender 2-4-0s and 2-2-2s to 2-4-0s, with some rebuilt as tank engines. These latter were not too successful and soon had their design altered again and tenders replaced.

The influence of Gooch was not sacrosanct, and by the early 1880s all of his designed locomotives of standard or 4ft 8½in gauge had been overtaken by replacement engines constructed at Wolverhampton to new and more powerful designs. Some Gooch 0-6-0s, which had originally been built as a later batch with Stephenson valve gear in place of Gooch's own, remained in service to the end of their careers with only minor alterations.

The late 1880s and early 1890s saw six of Joe Armstrong's 2-4-0s (the '439' Class, built at Swindon) removed from service and replaced by new construction at the Stafford Road Works, but the writing was on the wall as far as the importance of the Wolverhampton Works was concerned. Locomotives were getting bigger, and the shops and facilities were appearing relatively smaller.

The year 1889 saw the last new tender passenger engines, double-frame 2-4-0s, leave the Stafford Road Shops, and early in the 1890s the last goods-type tender engines followed suit. From then on tank engines were the order of the day, mostly 0-6-0 saddle-tank designs of that period. Still turned out, possibly even to Swindon designs and of identical class with a completely individual Stafford Road-type colour scheme, the locomotives from Stafford Road Works progressed up to the turn of the century and the approach of the Churchward period. The independent existence of the Stafford Road Works, which had really been tolerated in the era of Armstrong and Dean, was coming to an end, and Swindon was now coming to the fore in leaps and bounds.

The locos in the Wolverhampton shops were still those very varied designs, both new and inherited, and included those from those master builders Armstrong, Gooch and Dean, but the Swindon Belpaire firebox boilers were arriving for replacements. The Churchward standardisation era had arrived.

The inadequacies of the shops at Stafford Road were felt with the arrival of designs for the 2-6-2 side-tank locomotives. The new locos did not fit the facilities whichever way was tried. Bringing in components on the traverser was not a problem, but as the building progressed, it seemed the pits were not long enough – the crane could not lift in one go for wheeling, which had to be done piecemeal. Up and down, forward and back with bars and levers to get the wheels in was bad enough, but the loco, if completed, could not be removed from the shop. Buffers had to be removed, pony trucks came out, spare bits of track were assembled and the levering and pushing started all over again. Too big for the traverser, the almost completed loco was pushed and shoved over the traverser pit on makeshift track until a shunting loco could hook on and pull it clear. Only then could the removed items be replaced to actually finish the engine. Improvements were urgently required at Stafford Road.

Swindon had now come to the peak of importance. Standardisation of locomotive components was under way and improvements for Stafford Road Works had been shelved indefinitely. The year 1908 saw the last new locomotive from the works, which now had a more minor repairing role to fulfil for the foreseeable future.

Of course, there was more to the argument related to the Swindon/Wolverhampton development problem than just size of works. The obvious thing to do when something becomes too small is to expand, and that was the crux of the matter.

Following Gooch's death in 1889, the directors had given serious consideration to the fate of the remaining broad-gauge system, retained, possibly reluctantly, whilst its chief instigator and supporter still lived. The decision was inevitable and in three short years it had gone. It had then been proposed that with future organisation Swindon should be the manufacture and repairs home for carriage and wagon rolling stock, and repairs and maintenance to locomotives in the southern Great Western area whilst Wolverhampton should remain and be developed as the main construction and manufacturing base for all new locomotives and continued repair, along with facilities at Worcester, of the northern Great Western area locomotive stock.

The pros and cons of this proposal are very relevant to the discussion. Wolverhampton was in the middle of an industrial area. The necessities for a heavy industry such as locomotive building were already to hand. Coal and coke, iron and steel, and the key to it all, labour, were readily obtainable – the latter in already-trained quantity almost waiting on the doorstep for work.

With the Swindon site, which was literally miles from anywhere, everything would need to be brought in. There were no existing facilities for anything in this still mainly agricultural area. Coal, coke, iron, steel: it would all have to be transported, and manpower would need recruiting elsewhere, the latter the most difficult of the lot with very little surplus available locally and none of it already skilled.

Weighing up everything carefully, it became apparent that although usually key factors, none of the above was really the key element in forming a decision. The first requirement of expansion policies is space in which to expand. The Wolverhampton site was surrounded by developments of one sort or another and the owners of suitable land sited in the expansion area would not at first even consider selling. Swindon, on the other hand, was situated in an area of agriculture and available land in the right place, at the right price, was there for the asking. At Wolverhampton there was also the problem of removing a hill if expansion was to be achieved!

By the time the Wolverhampton proposals could go ahead after very long and difficult negotiations, the decision had already been made and Swindon had the green light for development.

The opening year of the century saw board approval for expansion at Swindon and Churchward had (whilst still under Dean's overall control during his, Dean's, last few years before retirement) prepared a 233,400sq ft (approximately 2.12 hectares) proposal for new fitting, machine and erecting shops.

These Shops were to be to the west of the main existing works and were to be an advance in design materials from those used for the older part of the works. The original wood, cast iron and stone of the earlier shops had changed to brick and cast iron during earlier developments, but the new shops, the 'A' Shop complex, would be of brick and steel.

The shops fitted together like an '⊔' the top of which was the 480ft × 165ft fitting and machine shop, and the two legs the erecting shop, 415ft × 306ft. The erecting section had eighty pits equally split into a pair of double bays with a traversing table down the centre of both, serving the twenty pits on each side of its track. The bays were separated by a fitting bench and stock area, and served by an electric/hydraulic 50-ton crane over each line of twenty pits.

The shops were spacious, airy and well lit by a north-facing 'sawtooth' glazed roof and as many peripheral wall windows as the structural design would stand. Gas lighting was provided throughout, supplied from the works' gas plant. Also included in the structure was a powerhouse and an area to be developed as a test plant for static tests on the locomotives.

So opened the new century with an expanded works at Swindon, the expansion only a part of the actual potential requirement into which events were to thrust the works as a whole. With Swindon Works becoming the key GWR centre, developments leaping ahead and powerful 4-6-0 locomotives under development, the years around 1905–06 were those of great importance to the company. Expansion was becoming evident everywhere within its sphere of influence. New routes and harbour developments flourished, tying ocean liners and sea travel to the expanding railway system, with increased passenger and mail connections from Fishguard on the west coast through to Paddington.

More traffic meant more expansion, which in turn meant more rolling stock, both new and repaired. To take some of the pressure off Swindon, the old Westbourne Park area where Gooch had had his office in the early days, and a reminder of broad gauge, disappeared in a flurry of activity and a new shed and shop complex appeared at Old Oak Common. Along with a new carriage shed and siding, accommodation was significantly increased at the London end of the system, but even so it was soon found to be not enough.

Expansion and updating, also at Swindon, was now essential. Within the decade locomotives had risen in weight and length to such an extent that the virtually new A shop was no longer adequate. The success of the 4-6-0, a great advance in Great Western locomotive design and certainly a pointer for other classes, meant that more of them were required than could be accommodated for construction, with anything approaching efficiency, in the existing shop.

The need for carriage and wagon stock replacements, due to new designs and increases in sizes, indicated that a joint review of the works as a whole was urgently required. A feature of the review by a business expert outside the railway sphere was to include the comparison of costs related to contractors and direct labour for building the new stock, tackling the locomotive side first.

The report concluded broadly that costs of home building were less than by contractors, but records and costing systems had not been as comprehensive as they could have been in arriving at these conclusions. Therefore, subject to certain limitations regarding building extensions, and the introduction of other improved costing methods, expansion was recommended.

The expansion was to make the A shop, as it then existed, into the largest and most comprehensive steam locomotive repair shop in Europe. On the western side of the existing shop were to be added in order of location (not necessarily order of construction), first a boiler bay with crane coverage and a special high section to deal with boiler shell riveting. Next, there was a locomotive erecting or maintenance section; two twenty-pit bays served by a traversing table running the length of the bays and through the outer doors to the tracks outside the shop. The long pits, if fully utilised, could accommodate eighty locomotives of any class.

Overhead, each bay of pits was served by a crane capable of lifting 100 tons, running the complete length of each bay. Being what was termed 'double crabbed', the cranes were capable of lifting and travelling with the heaviest locomotive above the rest under repair on the bay, the locomotive suspended from the heavy chains and steel ropes of the twin hoists on each crane.

Further west again, as a continued extension, stretched the area of wheel repairs where axles, wheels, tyres, lathes and wheel-balancing machines completely covered the floor space. In all, the complete shop covered over 11 acres under a continuous roof! I remember as an office boy and then as an apprentice in the shop, the sheer size of the shop, with steam locomotives wherever you looked, left an impression which has never faded. It will never be forgotten by anyone who witnessed it!

Similarly, the establishment of the locomotive test plant was under way, and again in later years to witness a 'Castle' travelling at 80mph yet going nowhere left an equally fixed, unforgettable impression – marvellous steam years!

Even the memory of the broad gauge lived on at Swindon right up to the end. Adjacent to the manager's office, in the original rectangle of the first shops, in the last few years of the life of the works removed from its position but still resting near its original location, was a small broad-gauge turntable. This had originally been sited outside the first boiler shop, later the G maintenance shop and still had its broad-gauge rails positioned outside of the standard 4ft 8½in track. This table now rests outside STEAM, the Museum of the GWR, established in the old R machine shop.

The Wolverhampton versus Swindon conflict was now well and truly over, with Swindon emerging as the dominant repair and manufacturing centre of the Great Western.

In the efforts toward the resurrection of steam, what of Swindon Works itself? From the 310 acres of its heyday and following the demolitions illustrated in this chapter, the works site has, at the time of writing, reduced to almost its 1846 size. Several surviving buildings, whilst being retained, are destined for other development.

On the site of the old A shop complex the only building remaining is actually the weighbridge, a glaring example of industrial archaeological vandalism at its worst. It was completely stripped out (the weighing equipment was still operational) and the building turned into a brewery and a pub! The weighing equipment was removed by volunteers, under pressure from the developers, I would suggest never to be seen again! The site is now surrounded by housing. The site of the B shop, which had become a car park is now filled by flats as a housing complex.

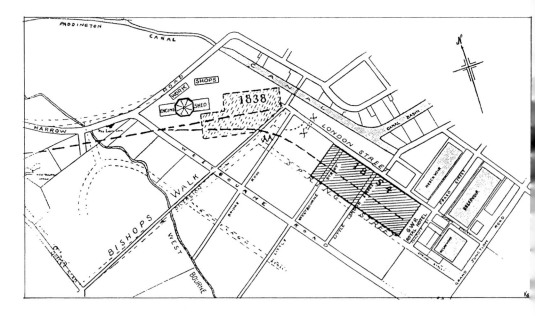

The early workshops at Paddington – 1838 and 1854.

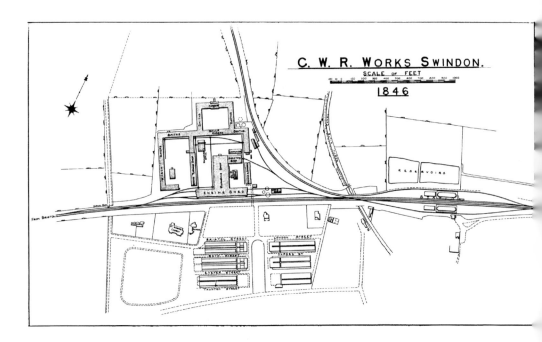

GWR Works, Swindon – 1846. They were built on open land with a housing estate for the workers. Note also the canal on the right of the works.

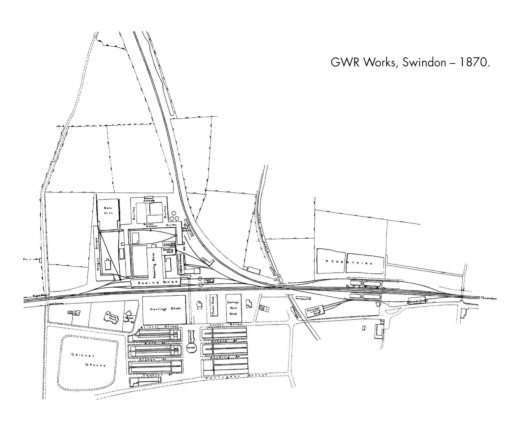

GWR Works, Swindon – 1870.

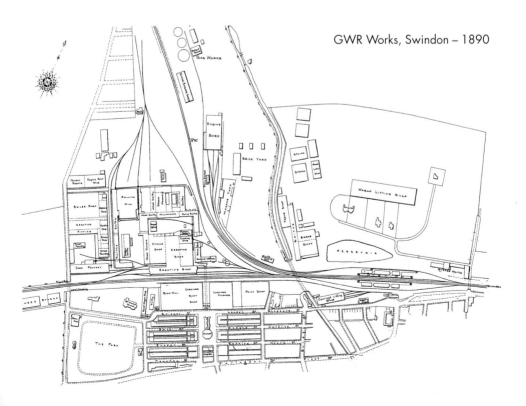

GWR Works, Swindon – 1890

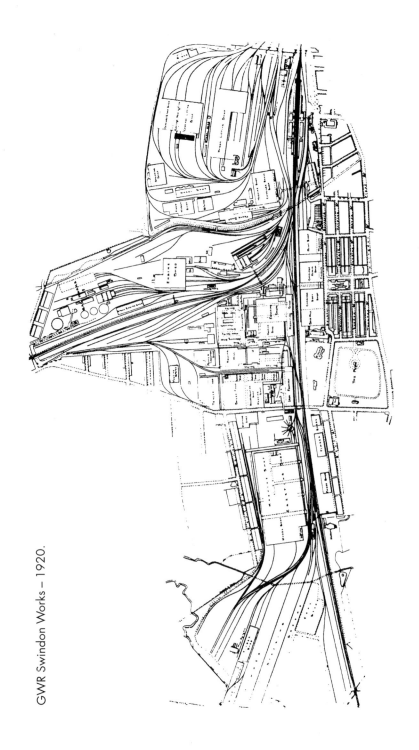

GWR Swindon Works – 1920.

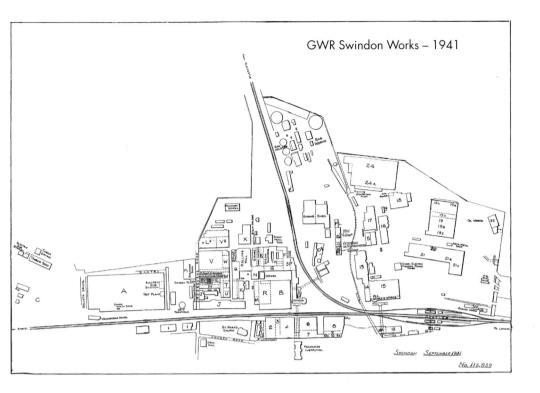

GWR Swindon Works – 1941

KEY:

Locomotive Shops

A	Erectors, boiler makers, painters & machine shop
B	Erectors, boiler makers, painters & tender shop
C	Concentration yard
D1	Carpenters
D2	Masons' yard
E	electrical shop
F & F2	Smiths, spring smiths & chain makers
G	Millwrights
H	pattern makers
J	Iron foundry
J2	Chair foundry
K	Coppersmiths & sheet-metal workers
L2	Tank shop
M	Electric substation
N	Bolt shop
O	Machine tools
P1	Boiler mounting
PL	Loco works roads & mains maintenance
Q	Angle ironsmiths
R	Fitters, turners & machinemen

S.P.	Spring smiths
T	Brass finishers
TH	testing house
U	Brass foundry
V	Boiler makers
V2	Tube cleaners
W	Turners & machinemen

Carriage & Wagon Shops

1	Sawmill west end
2	Sawmill
3	Fitting and machines
4	Carriage body building
5	Electric train lighting equipment
6	Carriage body repairs
7	Carriage finishing
8	Carriage painting
9	Carriage trimming
9A	Lining sewers
10	Laundry
10A	Polishers
11	General labourers
12	Carpenters
12A	Polishers
13	Wooden frame building

14	Smiths
15	Fitting and machines
16	Wheel shop
16A	Case hardening and normalising
17	Road vehicle building and repairing
18	Stamping
19	Carriage repairs
19A	Carriage trimmers repairs
19B	Carriage finishers repairs
19C	Carriage lifters
19D	Vacuum brake and carriage bogie repairs
20	Horse box and carriage truck repairs
21	Wagon building and repairs – wood section
21A	Wagon repairs – iron section
21B	Wagon painting
22	Oil and grease works
23	Platelayers' yard maintenance & breaking-up yard
24	Carriage paint repairs
24A	Carriage body repairs

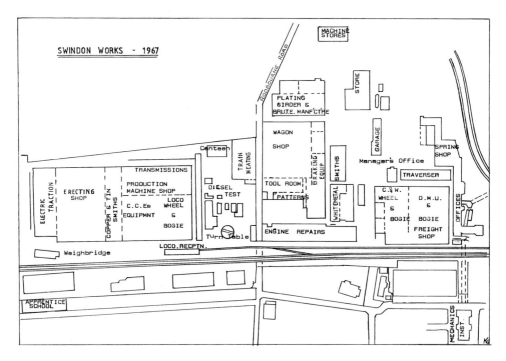

GWR Work Swindon – 1967. By this date steam had gone, and so had half the Swindon works. The locomotive works area now included the remnants of the carriage and wagon operations.

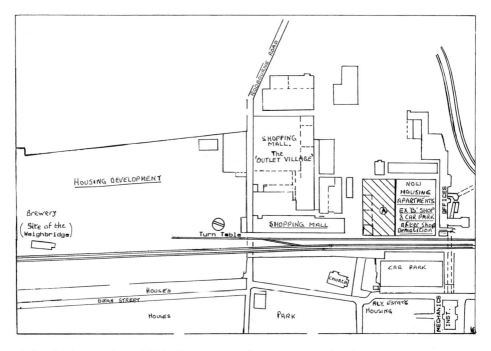

GWR Works Swindon – 2013. The structures that remain standing have an uncertain future, although some are proteceted. The shaded area is now STEAM, a railway museum centre for the GWR. The 'works' has returned almost to its 1843 area.

The first locomotive to steam on the GWR (shown here in 1858 converted and surviving in tank format).

Lagging a boiler – note lumps of old lagging set onto the new asbestos, which turned out to be a real killer.

A(V) boiler shop – the Iron Man riveter.

A view of the A(E) Shop, a frame with piston, springs and valve gear components in the foreground.

A view of the 'bosh' – the hot water and caustic soda component cleaning plant in the A(E) shop, Swindon.

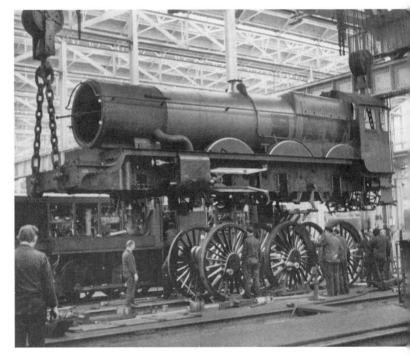

Preparing to wheel a 'Castle' in the A(E) shop, Swindon.

Swindon Works in the 1920s – note the flat-belt machinery drive.

A view of the boiler shop.

The pressing and flanging equipment in the boiler shop at Swindon Works.

The 'W' shop at Swindon. The cylinder boring bay – a regular sight. One of the machines shown is reputed to be an original from around 1850.

Kelham Hall 5904 with valves out at Swindon Shed. This work was not considered important enough to warrant official 'shopping' to the main works, and was carried out in the running shed itself on this occasion.

The valve-setting plant, A(E) shop in the 1950s. Press-button inching the wheels round. Locomotive shown on 'front dead centre' to set the valve. Without such plant (as with the small tank locos repaired in B shop) 'pinch bars' were used to move the loco backwards and forwards to set the valves.

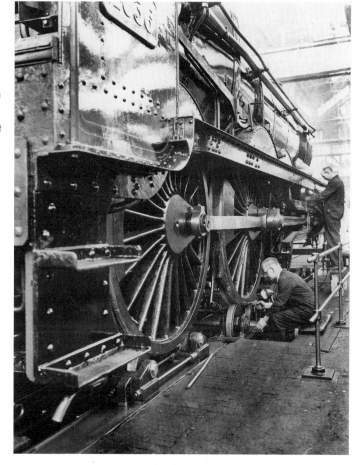

Setting the Valve on the A(E) shop valve-setting plant.

A posed photograph of work in the open. Fitting the axle boxes to the horns is evident along with work on the cylinders as both pistons are out. It is interesting to see the collars and ties and the bowler hats of the fitters filing the axle boxes. The men with the long bar and the screw jack are probably waiting to assist the fitters to jump or fit the boxes up into the horns (see also overleaf). Note: This photograph is reputedly at Swindon, but some authorities place it at Wolverhampton – 0-6-0 No. 35 was not a Swindon locomotive. However, it does show craftsmen of the period at work.

The original running shed at Swindon from which the B shed got its name.

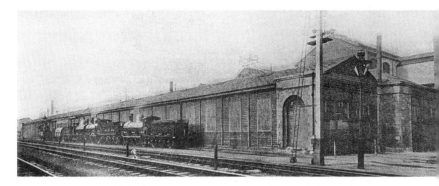

A(E) shop, Swindon Works. New construction with axle boxes being 'jumped' into the Horns (see also p.7642 – 1886).

Ready for or back from a test run in around 1953, *King Edward VII* waits outside the ash shed at Swindon, already fitted with the indicator shields.

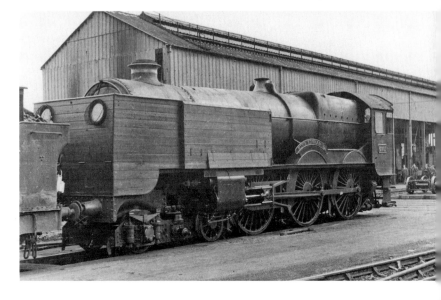

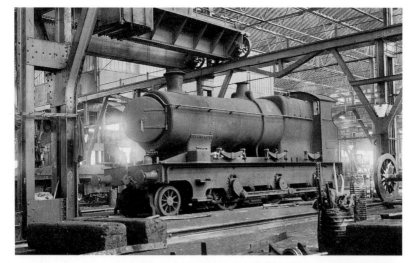

An 'Aberdare' 2-6-0 under the crane in the older section of Swindon's A(E) shop.

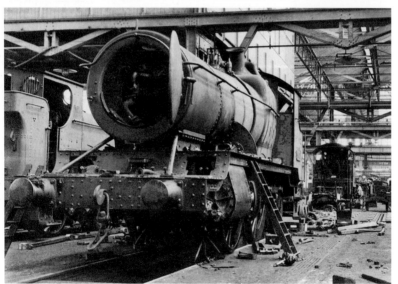

Intermediate repair in Swindon's A(E) shop (new extension).

A 'standard' and a GW design wait for repair in 1953 (and foul the straight road!) Unknown at the time but destined for a short life.

A last gasp of GW design and breaking the Churchward mould, a 1500 Class 0-6-0 pannier tank with outside cylinders and Walschaert valve gear takes on water.

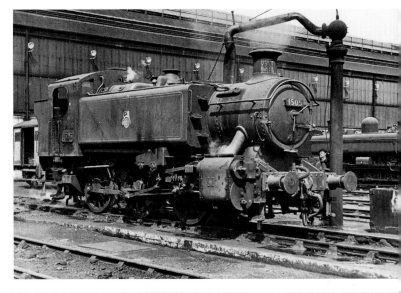

The fate of steam? An example of the proposed end of worldwide steam – these destined to be cut up at Swindon's C shop.

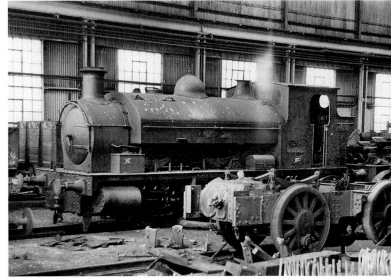

The cutting-up shed: was this to be the fate of GW steam? Victims of the oxytorch. Fortunately, there were survivors, now steaming again!

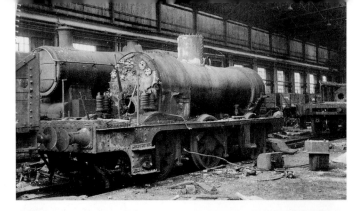

Locos partially stripped awaiting the oxytorch.

The abandoned A(E) shop – the end at Swindon Works.

The boiler shop, almost now emptied.

The stripped out brass foundry. The last days of the U shop at Swindon – 1988.

The shop stands empty – the sad fate suffered by most steam workshops.

The A(E) shop. End walls demolished, the 100-ton cranes were pulled off the end of their tracks and are here being oxy-cut for scrap.

The A(W) (wheel) shop has already gone and the A(E) shop awaits its turn.

2

The Stafford Road Works, Wolverhampton

With Swindon now firmly established as the hub of locomotive repair and manufacturing, the 1921 amalgamations put a large stick in the spokes! Again, the inadequacies of the area maintenance became apparent and although there were now lifting shops scattered throughout the system for repairs that could not be done by running sheds alone, or were not considered for shopping at main works, the system was once again overloaded.

The main burden of this programme was to be shouldered by the extended works at Caerphilly, but the opportunity to rehash the Wolverhampton Stafford Road Works, as we have seen, shelved for thirty years, was about to be taken. The works from its establishment in 1858 had grown piecemeal to cope with increasing demands, a difficult site making equally difficult the various processes required. Whilst it would still not be making, in the full sense, complete locomotives, that procedure had now been long established at Swindon, the facilities for repair could certainly be improved.

Due to its location in a nominally already built-up area, the works had developed split in two by a main road and, most awkwardly of all, was on two different levels. As always, financial as well as practical reasons were factors in such rebuilding or reorganising decisions and the Development (Loan Guarantees and Grants) Act of 1929 was a major factor in firstly, easing unemployment generally throughout the country, and secondly, giving the spur to a long-shelved idea. The main functions of locomotive repair, wheel and erecting work, were catered for in a brand new three-bay structure measuring about 450 × 200ft, two bays allocated to locomotive repairs and the third for wheels and general machine shop.

The new machine shop also required new machinery, contracts being placed during 1932 as follows:

Amount	Type	Company
1	Defries automatic keyway milling machine	Messrs Herbert, Coventry
1	Double spindle vertical hole grinding machine	Churchill Co., Manchester
1	Combination turret lathe – Independent Motor	Ward & Co., Birmingham
1	Lathe 10½in with independent motor drive	Messrs L. Long Co, Glasgow
3	Lathes 12½in with independent motor drive	
4	Lathes 10½in belt driven from counter shafting	
1	Lathe 12½in belt driven from counter shafting	
(All of the sliding, surfacing and screw-cutting type)		
1	Lathe 12½in raised to 31½in centre sliding and surfacing only	Messrs Darling & Sellers, Keighley
1	Oxy-cutting 55in machine	Messrs BOC, London
1	Locomotive frame cutting machine	
8	30hp electric motors	Messrs EC Co., Wolverhampton
1	Wheel lathe	Messrs Loudon Bros, Johnstone, Glasgow

This detail is included to indicate the spin-off work to other firms from the flourishing railway expansion and refurbishment orders. Although at a time of general depression, work was still to an extent being generated and assisted with maintaining order books and thus employment in other than the railway itself.

The erecting bays differed from those that existed at Swindon, and in the enlarged Caerphilly Works, in that it was an end-to-end system with two 50-ton overhead cranes in each bay, but the space for maybe a desirable side-by-side format and the usual traversing table was not really affordable within the shop itself. By the mid 1930s the new shop format was well established and operating.

The complete layout at Stafford Road, utilising the available space, was still not ideal as it was still a very roundabout route for locomotives from shop to shed or vice versa, and the works itself was still cut in half by the main Stafford road. Whilst the same could be said really about Swindon, itself cut into three, first by a main Rodbourne road, and by the remains of a canal, now a pedestrian way and cycle track, at least there was direct bridge access over all the obstacles straight into adjacent sections. There was also a tunnel under the road, which could take a complete boiler from the boiler shop to the mountings shop (P1 shop).

As with Great Western construction generally, as much as possible was homemade, and for Stafford Road, whilst obviously the brick structure had to be built where it was actually required, the steelwork of girders and roof principles was fabricated in the L2 shop at Swindon Works. The new shop, whilst differing in layout, was quite light and airy, and followed the general construction principles of Swindon's new A(E) shop extension. Original shops on the original side of Stafford Road (at least the originals were near the running sheds) were reallocated to other work. The old boiler, tender and tank repair shop became another running shed, the smiths' shop was now the lifting shop, and the new Road Motor Depot was housed in the paint shop. The coppersmiths' also crossed the road into an old boiler shop at the south end of the iron foundry, which took part of the shop to extend facilities. Into this shop also, retaining pits and a new traverser, moved the millwrights and repair of travelling cranes.

On the 'wrong' side of the road, where the new shop now stood and between it and the other two sides of a triangle formed by the line to Wolverhampton and the wall of the Stafford Road, was the new boiler shop. This now occupied the old wheel shop and related machinery and the old repair shop. A section of the old machine shop was allocated for pattern-making and carpenters' work, as well as a 'power' area to house air compressors and hydraulic pumps, and an electricity substation. Electrical power was supplied by the local authority, Wolverhampton Corporation. Also in the 'angle' was the forge and smiths' shop. All-in-all it was a very difficult shape and layout for a locomotive repair works.

The size of the works, its layout and its facilities still governed the nature of work to be carried out. New locomotive construction had long ceased, as previously mentioned, but the usual categories of repairs could be undertaken with stock coming from the general area as well as from the stock stationed at Stafford Road. The preset repairs classifications, already established over the system, were the 'light', 'intermediate' and 'heavy' or 'general' repair. The larger 'King' Class, whilst in the maintenance fleet at Stafford Road, could only be handled for the first two of the classifications, the facilities there not being suitable for the 'general', which had to be routed to Swindon. The bigger locos of the area were also not allowed to cross the Oxley Viaduct, although some crept over in the later years.

Rebuilt following the amalgamation, the works entered the war years within the same decade, to be followed by another change of ownership immediately following the successful conclusion of the conflict. The years of nationalisation had arrived. Having waited thirty years for recognition and rebuilding the new brand of locomotives of standard design still imposed the old limitations on the shops, but more serious events waited in the future. Within the next fifteen years steam itself would go and with it the need for any shops, whether old or new. Stafford Road Works closed on 1 June 1964.

Whilst the two main protagonists had eventually sorted themselves out, there were still a number of additional and historically important repair centres that seem to have been forgotten in the latter-day fixation on the power or influence of the Swindon Works. Although such power and influence must be acknowledged – indeed the association of Swindon Works with the GWR is inescapable in all contemporary literature – there were in the Great Western area at the end of its association with steam, both Great Western design and standard design, other well-established works and depots.

There existed seven major works, nine divisional works and thirty-seven lifting shops, which dealt with steam locomotive requirements ranging from running repairs to major overhauls.

These facilities had developed, or been established, during the course of the expansion of the company at various sites within the areas of absorbed railway companies, which themselves had become important constituents in the development of the GWR. The absorbed companies had, as independent operators, developed their own repair and manufacturing facilities, facilities which had sometimes grown – as had the Great Western's with the demands placed upon them as the companies themselves grew – although very few of them had actually established a complete manufacturing system. Only one, the works at Wolverhampton, Stafford Road, was to come anywhere near the manufacturing capacity and facilities of Swindon, finishing with a total of 794 locomotives completed – the last batch showing the inadequacies of the works – and actual new building ceasing in 1908.

Locomotive No. 14 was built by Sharp Bros in 1848. It was preserved at Wolverhampton works until 1918 when, like the Great Western's *North Star* and *Lord of the Isles*, it was destroyed because someone wanted the space, and an original Shrewsbury & Chester Railway relic disappeared.

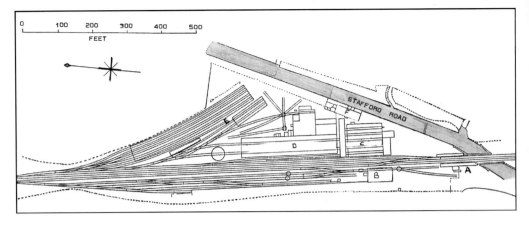

The Stafford Road headquarters of the Shrewsbury & Birmingham Railway c. 1849.

A Passenger stations & platforms (temporary)
B Goods station & yard (temporary)
C Repair shop & traversing table
D Locomotive shed
E Carriage & wagon sheds
F Offices

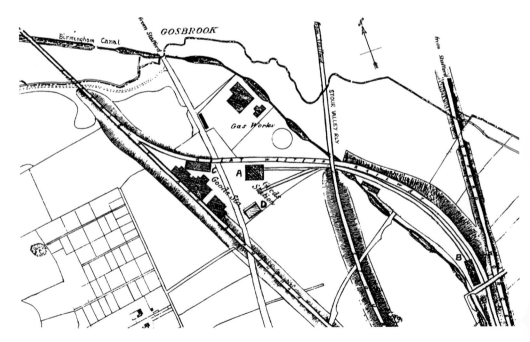

Broad-gauge loco yard at Stafford Road c. 1855 (taken from a legal document).

A Broad-gauge goods shed
B Thought to be a temporary engine shed
C Broad-gauge engine shed (contractor Branson & Gwyther at cost of £1,787) – tender accepted 1856, suspended 1857
D The accepted position of the broad-gauge shed authorised and completed in 1857

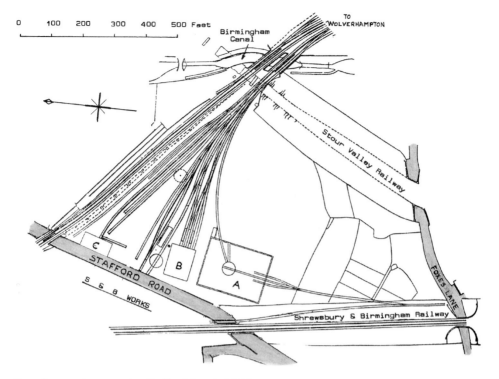

Broad-gauge loco yard at Stafford Road, 1860.

A Standard-gauge (4ft 8½in) shed, added 1860
B Broad-gauge shed
C Stores

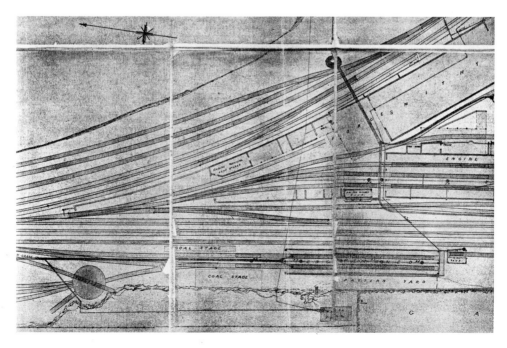

Wolverhampton, Stafford Road, 1867 (taken from a very flimsy re-backed plan).

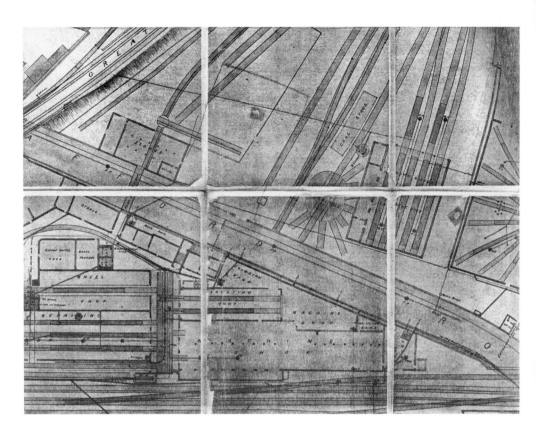

Wolverhampton, Stafford Road, 1867.

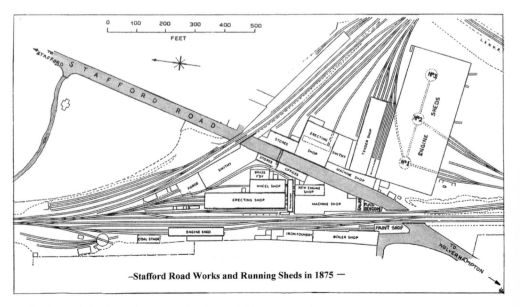

Stafford Road Works and running sheds in 1875.

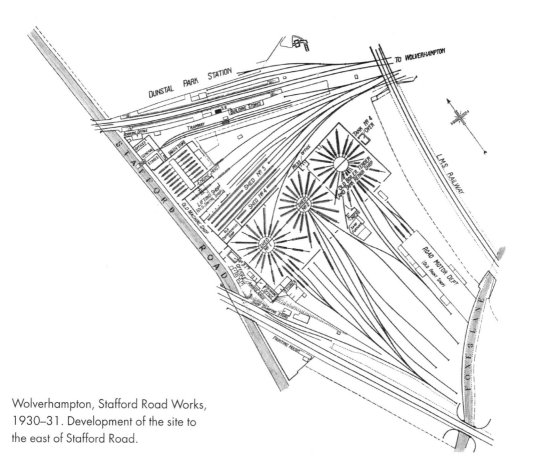

Wolverhampton, Stafford Road Works,
1930–31. Development of the site to
the east of Stafford Road.

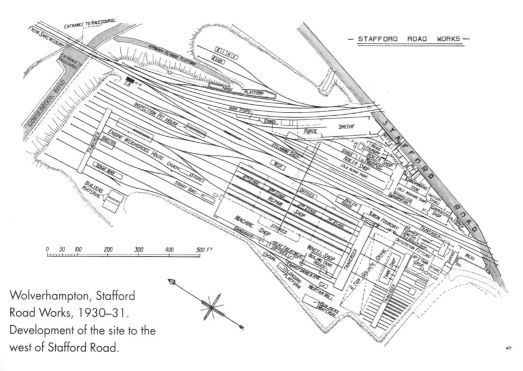

Wolverhampton, Stafford
Road Works, 1930–31.
Development of the site to the
west of Stafford Road.

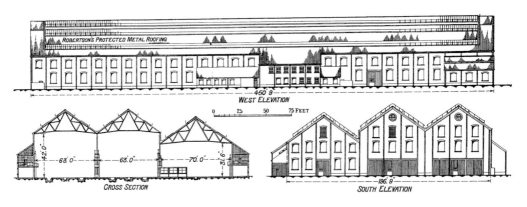

ROBERTSON'S PROTECTED METAL ROOFING

450' 9"

WEST ELEVATION

0   25   50   75 FEET

42' 0"

68' 0"   68' 0"   70' 0"   31' 6"

CROSS SECTION

196' 9"

SOUTH ELEVATION

Opposite top: Wolverhampton, Stafford Road Works. The 1930–31 erecting & machine shops.

Opposite centre: Stafford Road Works before rebuilding in 1930–31.

Opposite bottom: The new shop.

The engine erecting shop.

Machine shop under construction.

Tank shop and wheel yard.

Locomotive repair bay, looking north.

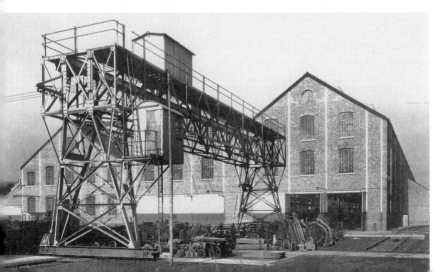

The parts yard and 6-ton crane.

Loco repair bay, looking south.

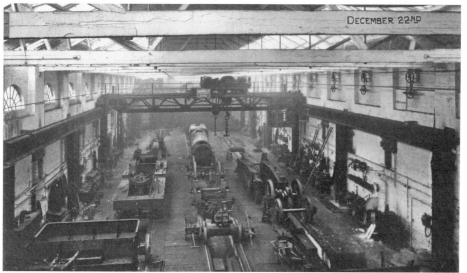

DECEMBER 22ND

Reconstructed boiler shop (former erecting shed).

The tank shop – tender and tank repairs. (What is the superheater header doing in the foreground?)

The foundry.

Reconstructed spring shop.

General view of new machine shop, Wolverhampton – 1932.

Machine fitting shop, Wolverhampton.

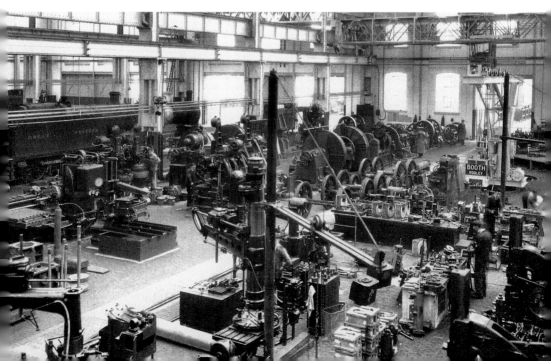

The machine shop.

Opposite top: In the erecting shop, Wolverhampton.

Opposite bottom: Stafford Road Works, Wolverhampton: a double 'roundabout'. Setting up an axle box.

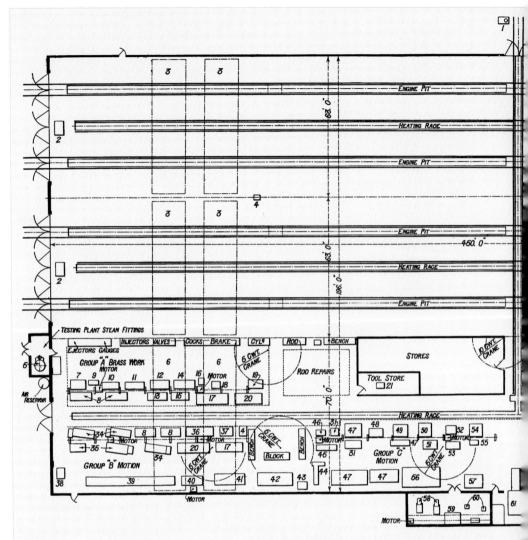

LIST OF MACHINE TOOLS AND OTHER EQUIPMENT IN REPA

1. 1-Ton Electric Capstan, Cowans, Sheldon & Co. Ltd.
2. 5-Ton Electric Winch, Cowans, Sheldon & Co. Ltd.
3. 50-Ton Overhead Electric Travelling Crane, Wharton Crane & Hoist Co. Ltd.
4. Grinders, Luke & Spencer Limited.
5. Boiler for Steam Fittings Testing Plant, Cochran & Co. (Annan) Ltd.
6. 6-Ton Overhead Electric Travelling Crane, Wellman, Smith & Owen Engineering Corporation Limited.
7. No. 7 Capstan Lathe, H. W. Ward & Co. Ltd.
8. 10-in. Lathe, John Lang & Sons Ltd.
9. Brass Lathe.

10. 8-in. Gap Lathe.
11. 10-in. Lathe, Sir W. G. Armstrong, Whitworth & Co. Ltd.
12. No. 7 Turret Lathe, H. W. Ward & Co. Ltd.
13. No. 7 Lathe, H. W. Ward & Co. Ltd.
14. No. 7 Combination Lathe, H. W. Ward & Co. Ltd.
15. No. 5A Lathe, Alfred Herbert Limited.
16. Grindstone, Churchill Machine Tool Co. Ltd.
17. Lathe, Darling & Sellers Limited.
18. Radial Drill, Jones & Shipman Limited.
19. Drill, Craven Bros. (Manchester) Ltd.
20. 12½-in. Lathe, John Lang & Sons Ltd.
21. Twist Drill Grinder, Herbert Hunt & Son.
22. 10½-in. Lathe, John Lang & Sons Ltd.
23. 4-ft. Radial Drill, Wm. Asquith (1920) Limited.

24. Cylinder Level Plate.
25. No. 3 Borer, H. W. Kearns & Co. Ltd.
26. Universal Cutting Machine, British Oxygen Ltd.
27. Axle Box Borer, Webster & Bennett Limite
28. Boring Machine, Webster & Bennett Limite
29. Wheel Lathe, Craven Bros. (Manchester) Ltd.
30. Hydraulic Wheel Press, Fielding & Platt Limi
31. Lapping Machine, G.W.R.
32. Crank Turning Machine, Craven Bros. (M chester) Ltd.
33. Quartering Machine, Cunliffe & Croom Lim
34. Turret Lathe, Alfred Herbert Limited.
35. No. 4 Capstan Lathe, Alfred Herbert Limit
36. 12-in. Lathe.

General plan drawing of new locomotive erecting and machine shops, Wolverhamp

Typical layout of steam loco erecting and machine shop.

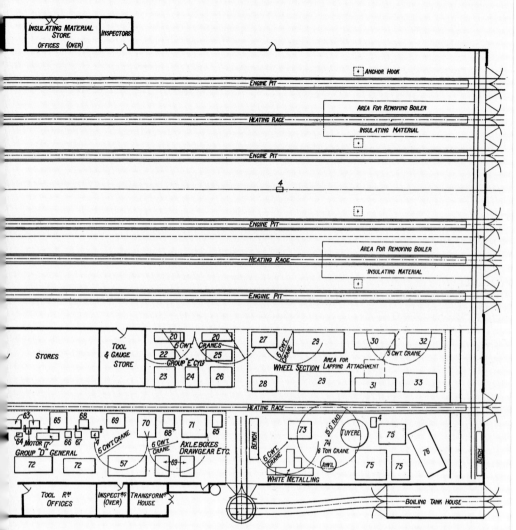

PS AT WOLVERHAMPTON LOCOMOTIVE WORKS, G.W.R.

Centering Machine, John Lang & Sons Ltd.
Magnetic Separator, J. W. Jackman.
12-in. Gap Lathe, Tangyes Limited.
Lathe, Beyer, Peacock & Co. Ltd.
No. 10 Turret Lathe, H. W. Ward & Co. Ltd.
Piston Rod Grinder, Ludwig Loewe & Co. Ltd.
Heat Treatment Furnace, Incandescent Heat Co. Ltd.
Broaching Machine, Lapointe Machine Tool Co. Ltd.
Press.
Press, Burton, Griffiths & Co. Ltd.
Grinding Machine, Churchill Machine Tool Co. Ltd.
Slot Drilling Machine, Tangyes Limited.
Vertical Milling Machine, Wm. Muir & Co. Ltd.

50. Vertical Milling Machine, Alfred Herbert Limited.
51. Drill, Defries.
52. Horizontal Miller, Parkinson & Son.
53. Key Seater, Smith & Coventry (1927) Limited.
54. Planer, Ward Haggas & Smith.
55. Shaper, Smith & Coventry (1927) Limited.
56. Duplex Shaper, Butler Machine Tool Co. Ltd.
57. Shaper, Butler Machine Tool Co. Ltd.
58. Grinder, John Lund Limited.
59. Grinder, The Lumsden Machine Co. Ltd.
60. Buff, G.W.R.
61. Case-Hardening Furnace, Incandescent Heat Co. Ltd.
62. Cutter Grinder, Alfred Herbert & Co. Ltd.
63. Screwing Machine, Landis.

64. Tap Grinder, Herbert Hunt & Sons.
65. Radial Drill, Columbia.
66. Saw, Chas. Wicksteed & Co. Ltd.
67. Drill, Colburn.
68. Radial Drill, Kitchen & Wade Limited.
69. Slotter, Butler Machine Tool Co. Ltd.
70. Radial Drill, Wm. Asquith (1920) Limited.
71. Radial Drill, James Archdale & Co. Ltd.
72. Hiloplaner and Veloplaner, John Stirk & Sons Ltd.
73. Tyre Rolls, B. & S. Massey Limited.
74. 6-Ton Jib Crane, J. Booth & Bros. Ltd.
75. Tyre Boring Machine, Cravens Bros. (Manchester) Ltd.
76. Wheel Stripping Lathe, Loudon Bros. Ltd.

orks, Great Western Railway, showing disposition of machine-tool installation

Stafford Road Works machine shop layout & machine tool groups

GROUP A

N° on Plan	Reg & N°	Machine	Duty
7	A 2555	No. 7 Ward capstan lathe	Injector parts
8	A 2159	10in Lang lathe	Steam & feed cocks – pump & hyd parts
9	A 371	Adapted brass lathe	Steam & air valves, spindle & piston glands
10	A 2073	8in Willson gap lathe	Clacks, steam cocks
8	A 2158	10in Lang lathe	Ejectors, steam cocks
12	A 1217	No. 7 Ward turret lathe	Motion bushes
	A 2558	No. 10 Ward turret lathe	Con & coup: rod bushes
13	A 2557	No. 7 Ward turret lathe	Con & coup: rod bushes
14	A 2556	No. 7 Ward turret lathe	Injector & ejector parts
	A 1228	No. 5A Herbert lathe	Motion bushes
16	F 1138	Churchill grindstone	Precision tools
18	B 1177	2ft 3in Jones & Shipman radial drill	Motion pins, bushes & liners, brake gear
17	A 2328	12½–31½in Darling & Sellers Lathe	Brake & rev: shafts, crank axles
19	B 426	Craven fixed drill	Con & coup: rods, s'heater headers
20	A 2156	12½in Lang lathe	rod brasses, Vac: piston & heads, valve rods
11		10in 'Armstrong' Whitworth lathe	

GROUP B

N° on Plan	Reg & N°	Machine	Duty
	L 152	Jackman magnetic separator	Swarf
35	A 1287	No. 4 Herbert capstan lathe	Pins, bolts, studs, bushes
34	A 2532	No. 3 Herbert turret lathe	Bolts, studs, pins
35	A 1219	No. 4 Herbert capstan lathe	Motion pins, brake & spring bushes
34	A 2531	No. 3 Herbert turret lathe	Bolts, studs, pins
29	A 1062	12in Tangye gap lathe (2 heads)	S'heater tubes, crane & turntable shafts
8	A 2160	10in Lang lathe	Vac: pump rods & covers, pistons, Xheads, G pins
34	A 1284	No. 13 Herbert turret lathe	Bolts, pins, studs
8	A 2161	10in Lang lathe	Crank pins, brake & draw gear, valve spindles

20	A 147	12½in Lang lathe	Pistons
36	A 161	12in Whitworth lathe	Piston heads
37	A 1310	Lang centring machine	General
17	A 284	13½in Darling & Sellers lathe	Xheads, slide blocks, pony C pins & bkts, cyl covers
4	F 1199	36in Luke & Spencer grindstone	Precision tools
42	F 404	Ludwig Loeve Rod grinder heat treatment furnace	Piston rods, valve spindles, shafts. motion & c
41		No. 10 Ward & Co turret lathe	

GROUP C

N° on Plan	Reg & N°	Machine	Duty
44	C 551	La Point broach No. 4	Piston keyholes
46	R 1006	9½in D x 7½in S 1,500lbs Burton Griffiths Hor: Hyd: press	Pistons & Xheads bkt bushes, motion broach, bush press
31	B 186	GWR lapper	Motion
47	F 625	Churchill plain cylinder grinder	Motion pins & bolts, Short rods
31	A 351	GWR lapper	Motion
	F 576	Churchill vertical surface grinder	Slide bars, quad: links
47	F 521	Churchill grinder	Quad: links, con & coup: rods, motion
21	F 955	Hunt twist drill grinder	Drills
48	B 411	Tangye slot drill	Valve spindles, con: rod bolts
50	D 727	Herbert 'Graffenstaden' vertical miller	Motion axle boxes, Xheads, valve bkts
47	F 613	6in Churchill universal grinder	Motion, tools
	D 710	Herbert vertical miller	Con & Coup: rod brushes
51	D 432	Herbert Schess Defries key seat miller	All key seats
56	C 339	24in Butler duplex shaper	Valve bkts, pony horns, brake piston & gear
52	D 820	Parkinsons horizontal miller	Axle boxes, tools, motion
53	C 404	Smith & Coventry key seater	Pistons, valve spindles, shafts
49		W Muir & Co vertical milling m/c	
54	C 27	Ward Haggis & Smith 18in open slide planner	Xheads, valve bkts

	C 713	20in Smith & Coventry planer	Con: rod brasses, axle boxes
57	C 97	16in Butler shaping	Tools, cotters, keys
55	C 342	Smith & Coventry shaping	Squares, polygons
58	F 1027	40in Aloxite lund grinder	General
58	F 1040	40in Aloxite lund grinder	General
59	F 1226	Lumsden tool grinder	Machine tools
60	F 243	GWR buff	motion, Con & coup: rods
60	F 242	GWR buff	motion, Con & coup: rods
61		Case hardening furnace	Motion, shafts, decarbonising

GROUP D

N° on Plan	Reg & N°	Machine	Duty
62	F 509	Herbert cutter grinder	Milling cutters, taps, reamers
63	E 205	Landis screwer	Bolts, nuts, hangers, draw gear
64	F 1573	Hunt tap grinder	Reamers, rosebits, taps
63	E 858	Landis screwer	Bolts, studs
17	A 21	9in Darling & Sellers lathe	Tools
72	C 957	4 × 4 × 2ft Stirk planer (Hilo)	Frame plates, horn blocks, valve guides
65	B 1113	2ft 3in Cincinatti radial drill	Frame plates, angles
66	D 222	Wicksteed saw	Bars, angles
67	B 44	Colburn fixed drill	Plates, angles
72	C 53	3 × 3 × 8ft Stirk planer (Velo)	Axle boxes, slide valves
71	B 1173	2ft3in radial drill (Archdale)	Pins, bolts, studs, axle box liners
4	F 1206	Luke & Spencer grinder	Tools
69	C 571	12in Butler slotter	Con: rod straps, horn, blocks, motion
	C 343	24in Butler shaper	Axle boxes
70	B 1648	4ft0in Asquith radial drill	Motion, brake & spring gear
68	B 1176	3ft0in Kitchen & Wade radial drill	Axle boxes
69	C 572	14in Butler slotter	Axle boxes, crown brasses, reg: boxes
69	C 565	14in Butler slotter	Rev: quadrants, axle boxes, crown brasses
71	B 1471	4ft6in Archdale radial drill	Shafts, horn blocks, angles, cylinders

GROUP E

N° on Plan	Reg & N°	Machine	Duty
20	A 145	12½in Lang lathe	Piston valve sleeves SB cylinders
22	A 2155	10½in Lang lathe	Brake pistons, bkts, bushes, Con: R brasses
23	B 1469	4ft Asquith radial drill	Motion, brake & spring gear
24		Cylinder level plate	
68	B 1174	3ft Kitchen & Wade radial drill	General
20	A 146	12½in Lang lathe	Draw & brake gear, glands, bushes
25	B 266	No 3 Kearns borer	Pumps, cylinders, capstans
26	L 189	BO Co profile cutter	Plates, blocks
27	A 1854	Webster & Bennett axle box borer	Axle boxes
28	A 1853	Webster & Bennett borer (4ft0in table)	Cylinders, eccentric straps, tyres
	R 1007	3½in × 12in × 1,500lb hydraulic press	Axle crown liners
73	E 924	Massey tyre rolls	Wheel tyres
		White metalling bench	General
29	A 1568	Craven wheel lathe	Wheels
29	A 1569	Craven wheel lathe	Wheels
		Tyring tuyere	Wheels
		Tyring anvil	Wheels
30	R 58	Fielding & Platt hydraulic wheel	Wheels, axles, pins
31	A 589	GWR lapper (press)	Wheel journals
4	F 1204	Luke & Spencer grinder	Tools
75	A 1852	Craven tyre borer	Tyres 4ft 4in–5ft 9in
75	A 731	Craven tyre borer	Tyres 5ft 9in–6ft 9in
32	A 2503	Craven crank turning lathe	Crank journals
33	A 749	Cunliffe & Croon quartering	Crank pins
76	A 1570	Loudon wheel skeleton lathe	Wheels
75	A 730	Craven tyre borer	Tyres 3ft 1in–4ft 2in

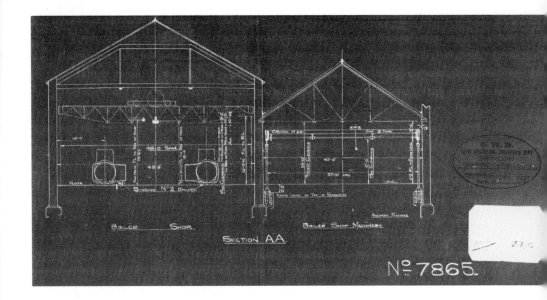

Stafford Road Works, Wolverhampton – 1932. Cross-section through the new boiler shop – boiler and machinery bays.

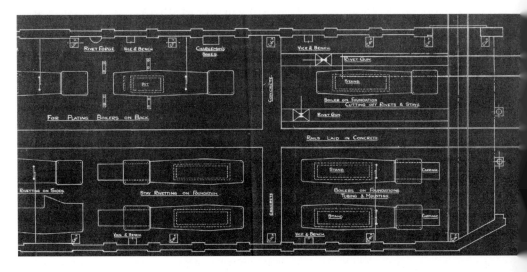

Stafford Road Works, Wolverhampton – 1932. Plan view (part) of new boiler shop layout.

Stafford Road Works, Wolverhampton. Grinding a reversing gear 'link' or 'quadrant'.

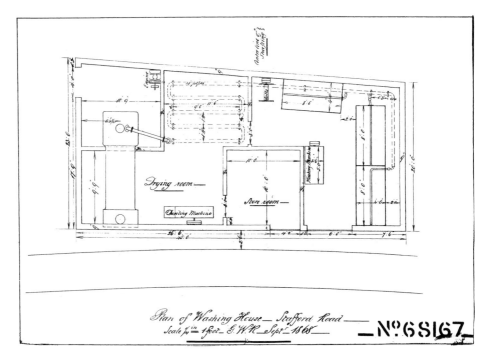

Plan of washing house, Stafford Road Works, Wolverhampton (scale ¼in = 1ft). GWR, September 1868, No. 68167.

The end of Stafford Road Works, 1964.

PART 3

1

Taff Vale Workshops, West Yard, Cardiff Docks, 1845–1926

At the time when the Great Western Swindon Works was being constructed, away to the west in the Welsh valleys the railway fever was already strongly endemic. The expansion of coal production triggered and emphasised the need for the new mechanical steam transport system, and the first Welsh railway company came into being, its later absorption by the Great Western still eighty years in the future.

As with virtually all new railways, the Taff Vale Railway had no facilities at its birth for the production of its rolling stock and, again in keeping with others in a similar position, the first orders were given to the known contractors of the day. The problem was immediately apparent, in that if a specification is given to several different builders, then several different interpretations will emerge, giving many problems to those having to run and maintain such products. Some maintenance may be done in the open air, but covered workshops are really the answer and when, as with other companies, a build-it-yourself force exerts itself, then a proper construction workshop is essential. At West Yard a small dock was built adjacent to the Glamorganshire Canal to facilitate the supply of materials to the works site.

A site that looks ideal at the start very rapidly loses its charm when a later development is planned and it is then found impossible to increase the original area. The Taff Vale was no exception and the board found itself landed with such a site. Stuck between a main road and a canal, the first snag was that the access was across Bute Street, the main road from the dock's station, and horses had to be employed to move everything to and fro.

At the start in 1840 the locomotive superintendent took up his duties with enthusiasm but soon found that maintenance problems increased with every new locomotive from the makers. The 'super' stayed a year and his successors very little longer, a total of seven being employed up to 1858!

A first rebuild, although classified as a new locomotive, was a Sharp Roberts & Co. 0-4-2, which was made into an 0-6-0 in 1841; a nearly new engine to start with which highlights the problems of some of the early designs and manufacture.

Venus sprang from the waves of the erecting shop in 1857 and was the first genuinely new locomotive built at the Works, a 2-4-0 with 4½ft-diameter wheels and 14½in × 20in cylinders. Both the rebuild, named *Cardiff*, and *Venus* had double frames and these and subsequent engines with double frames were all prone to axle breakage due to the too-rigid support of the extra axle boxes – a feature of the double frame generally and not a workmanship fault.

A number of contract firms were still used, although construction continued at the works, including in 1864, two passenger 2-4-0s, again with double frames, and this time 5ft-diameter wheels. The main traffic into and out of the valleys was the mineral wealth, and passenger traffic was only really of secondary importance. The coal traffic at this time was some of the most prolific 'goods' transport in the country, a continual movement of full trucks and returning empties.

Locomotive sizes continued to increase generally. In the mid 1880s three 4-4-0 tank engines were built for branch line use and auto working. The last type in the development cycle came in 1891 when the 0-6-2T appeared from the shops, following a batch of similar engines by Kitson Company, making a total of thirty-eight in all. The 0-6-2 format continued with an improved batch with slight dimensional changes, giving greater overhang at the front end, but by now the stock had reached requirements. These latter '01' Class included eight by Kitson Company in 1894, and six built at the works in 1897. Building of locos at West Yard came to an end with the last of the batch, but steam rail motor units were built early in the 1900s, eighteen completed and running in a quite extensive use of this hybrid form of transport – part locomotive, part passenger coach.

With the increase in locomotive sizes came the old problem, as experienced at Wolverhampton, of the locos not fitting in with the rest of the facilities. The traversing tables, essential for the internal movement between and into the workshops were becoming too small. The platforms slung on eight wheels were not long enough for the 0-6-2 designs, being built for virtually nothing bigger than the six-wheel arrangements of the early years. Movement was by manual lever inserted in indents cast into the traverser table wheels, four levers giving manual propulsion per side. Levers (or pinch bars) also gave movement onto and off the tables, and in and out of the shops. To get even an 0-6-2 onto a table meant lifting and dropping the trailing wheels making an overlong 0-6-0.

By the turn of the century, the West Yard had developed by about as much as it possibly could and a review of facilities was urgently required. A superb model of the works (see p.77) was made by Mr D. Taylor, who with great precision illustrates the full utilisation of every inch of available space on site in the years around 1900. The use of the small dock also reduced as the new century opened. In 1916 the dock was filled in, and whilst giving an increased area for other development, it was really too late anyway bearing in mind the other limitations of the site.

Interrupted by the First World War, the Taff Vale expansion plans relating to workshop facilities were shelved. There was absolutely nowhere to go anyway on the West Yard site and proposals for a new works at Radyr came to nought, stifled after the war by absorption of the company by the Great Western in the 1921 amalgamations.

A new dimension had now entered the problem field and the horizons were much wider than just the Taff Vale Railway environs. Land was available at the Caerphilly Works of the Rhymney Railway, and the Taff Vale Works were allowed to run down, ceasing repairs in 1926 on transfer to the new site at Caerphilly.

On closure in 1926 the site was cleared and all buildings demolished, lying idle for several years, being caught in the depression period of the late 1920s and early '30s. Some housing was eventually erected, but the railway use ended with the closure and transfer of work to Caerphilly.

The fleet of 274 locos taken over by the Great Western included eighty-four directly associated with the West Yard Works, either built or rebuilt, which really amounted to almost new locomotives. Contractors over the years had supplied the rest of the fleet, and those built at the works itself had mostly followed the contractors' drawings and designs. There were exceptions and locomotives designed by the largest standing and possibly most influential of the superintendents, Tom Hurry Riches (1873–1911) were built in conjunction with Kitson Company. Most were built by a Kitson contract but twelve were completed at the West Yard Works.

With no iron foundry or very heavy facilities, large components would have been supplied by contractors. This was probably the case for the three 4-4-0s built in the 1880s; a design with similarities to those built for the Monmouthshire Railway & Canal Company. With 16in × 24in cylinders and 5ft 3in drivers, sizes not too big to handle in the heavy machine shop, the complete loco weighed about 45½ tons.

About two dozen engines built at the works survived until the amalgamation, but by 1930 all had been withdrawn.

This is not quite the end of the locomotive story, however. One of the last batch built in 1897, No 28 (which had run a total of almost 484,000 miles), had been thoroughly overhauled on takeover and was in such good condition on withdrawal in 1926 that it was offered for sale. From government use on the Longmoor Military Railway by the first purchasers, who ran it for about twenty years, it was eventually sold to the Coal Board. After almost another two decades, it was finally withdrawn in 1960. As the only engine to survive from the Taff Vale fleet, its uniqueness ensured preservation following several moves, including a sojourn at the Caerphilly Works, itself awaiting closure. The predecessor of the current Caerphilly Railway Society leased the erecting shop at the closed works for a short period to 1969 and it is thus that No. 28 is claimed as the last steam locomotive to leave Caerphilly Works!

All of the stock and many staff had transferred to Caerphilly on closure of West Yard, Cardiff in 1926.

No. 28 is now preserved and running as part of the National Collection, its restoration and running under the auspices of the Caerphilly Railway Society, a unique reminder of the Taff Vale Railway, fiercely independent until directed into the clutches of the Great Western in 1921.

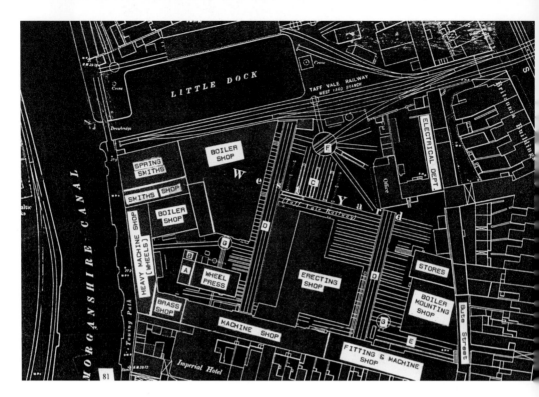

The Cardiff West Yard Workshops of the Taff Vale Railway, *c*. 1900.

Key
A Coppersmiths
B Brass foundry
C Overhead cranes (35 tons)
D Loco traversing tables
E Wagon traversing table
F Loco turntable
G Wagon turntable

Opposite: These three photographs are of a superb model of the works made by Mr D. Taylor.

Top: The locomotive (left) and wagon (bottom) traversing tables, both manually operated.

Centre: The difficulties of access to the works site. Note the horses moving locomotive across the main road into the workshops.

Bottom: The turntable and outside lifting arrangements. The overhead cranes were later 'boxed in' by the building shown in the photograph below.

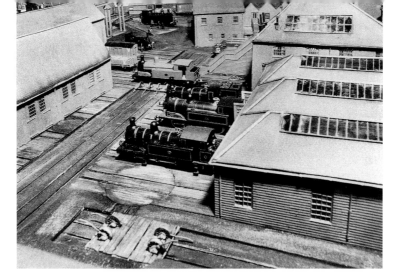

The hand-operated traversing table outside the lifting bay.

The machine section for wheels (1920s) at West Yard.

Cardiff (West Yard) Shops (c. 1925) of the late Taff Vale Railway. Eighty-four locos were built here. Note the absence of overhead lifting crane facilities, and that the benches have drawers or flaps instead of cupboards, but the ubiquitous 'leg vise' is in evidence.

The spring smiths' shop, *c.* 1920.

Queen Street offices of the Taff Vale Railway, Cardiff.

2

The Bristol and Exeter Railway Workshops

About a year after the birth of the GWR, indeed even possibly inspired by it, another group of worthy citizens of Bristol decided they too would become involved in this newfangled idea of steam railways. Eliciting the services of the Great Western's I.K. Brunel, who deputed one of his assistants to the task, a quick survey was done, a route from Bristol to Exeter mapped out and a Bill presented for Parliamentary approval.

The Bill had a much easier passage than did the raising of the necessary cash. The first flood of enthusiasm for the shares was not reflected when it came to finally paying for them, and whilst the directors attempted to woo those who had agreed to purchase into actually parting with their money, a cold financial draught was felt by the company. There were a few objectors to the proposal concerning the route, these mainly from canal companies and a handful of landowners. The latter quickly agreed when protective clauses were added to the proposal; the canal owners remained unhappy about the project – with some justification, as it turned out.

In the early months, indeed in the first few years, there was more speculation with share dealing than there was actually construction of the railway. Almost one-third of the issued shares were forfeited due to non-payment! Some preparation of the route had started in various places, but it was not until 1839 that the positive decision relating to the gauge was made and put directly to the shareholders. There was, inevitably, some opposition, but the company adopted the 7ft gauge.

Positive construction was under way at last. Materials such as rails and timber were ordered in bulk and a first purchase of the motive power put in hand. The Manchester firm of Sharp Roberts & Co. received an order for five locomotives. Finances were still a little shaky, however, and at a meeting held in 1840 the decision was made to lease the railway to Great Western, thus avoiding motive power and rolling stock costs, and its first twenty-eight locomotives, twenty passenger and eight goods, were designed by Gooch.

These first locomotives were to be built by contractors and the names of Stothert and Slaughter and Longridge & Co. of Bedlington are again recorded in the construction of locomotives with Great Western associations. One locomotive, which worked the Tiverton Branch and was certainly not a Gooch design, was built by a rather obscure contractor whose existence seems to fade out about 1860 but who produced in around 1848–49 some of the early 'rail motor' units comprising a steam power unit and a coach.

The firm of W. Bridges Adams opened in London in 1843, the proprietor already an innovator with a range of books and designs for a patent rail joint, as well as a radial axle box to his credit. He appears to have built about seven locomotives of various designs, the unit for the Bristol & Exeter having reputedly been built to standard gauge, possibly for the Eastern Counties Railway. It was converted to the 7ft gauge before sale and had an open power unit with a single-cylinder engine and a vertical boiler. Its drive was of the indirect form through an intermediate crank axle to coupled 4ft 6in driving wheels. Wheels of 3ft 6in supported an almost 32ft-long coach which held 48 passengers, but as with similar units in the future it was separated on rebuilding in 1851 and the engine unit became an 0-2-2 tank. It was sold out of the company in 1856.

Bristol & Exeter machinations involving other companies included an argument with the Taw Vale Railway, extending a dispute related to gauge problems that endured over several hard years. The Bristol & Exeter had nominally been run by stock from the Great Western and, having fought its own battles with other railway and canal companies, began to flex its muscles a little; its board of directors refused to be influenced by other controlling bodies, under lease or not, and any controls real or imagined imposed by the Great Western faded out.

More contracts were let out for locomotives, carriages and wagons, and coke ovens and carriage repair shops were laid out at Bridgwater, to take over as a repair centre, the construction of carriages and wagons, as well as repairs, commencing in 1848. The general repairs to the locomotives were dealt with at the Exeter running sheds, in anticipation of the full facilities being provided at Bridgwater.

Without the Great Western influence and with new posts established for administration, the company looked forward to some of the prosperity which they felt had been milked off by the Great Western during the leasing agreement. In 1850 the locomotive department was taken over by a new superintendent, James Pearson, who had the rather unique background of having been superintendent of the atmospheric system on the South Devon Railway. At his appointment he had been in charge of disposing of the remaining atmospheric ephemera, a memorial to a system in advance of materials and technology of the period – a problem which had caused its downfall. (£50,000 was recovered from material sales out of the £426,368 initial outlay.)

Drawings had been prepared for the construction of permanent Bristol & Exeter loco repair shops at Exeter but these were shelved, probably on the recommendation of the new superintendent for a site at the other end of the railway at Bristol. At the end of 1851, according to the report:

The new locomotive workshops at Bristol have been completed and the locomotive establishment removed from Exeter. The various machinery is now being fixed and a well sunk, which promises to yield a good supply of water, so that in a few weeks more we shall have as complete and inexpensive an Establishment of the kind as there is in the Kingdom.

Even this new works was quickly seen to be inadequate for the purpose, and only a matter of a year and a half later an expansion programme was in full swing. The new Locomotive Department and the already well established Carriage & Wagon Works were to run as separate establishments for the next twenty years. Also in the building programme for the 1850s was the construction of new main offices for the company, attached to the rail terminus at Bristol.

During the first five years or so that the new buildings were being erected no new engines were constructed, but some quite extensive rebuilding was undertaken as well as the routine repairs. James Pearson soon got to grips with the situation and set about designing his locomotive fleet. His first, a 4-2-4T, left the shops in September 1859, a forerunner of later designs, in this case with 7ft 6in drivers, but it was not until two and a half years later that a sister locomotive was out-shopped. Progress was slow and another four years passed before a solitary 0-6-0 saddle tank was completed, with a second completed the year following. There was certainly a contractor involvement with the supply of various components.

During 1868, possibly the most outstanding of Pearson locomotives appeared from their own shops, being renewals of the standard type peculiar to the Bristol & Exeter. A batch of three monsters was completed, being among the oddities always commented on by historians of railway doings – this author being no exception! These were 4-2-4 well and back tank locomotives replacing some of similar design built in the 1850s by Rothwell & Co. of the Union Foundry, Bolton. As unusual locomotives, there is almost a touch of Crampton about them, and the size differences when comparing these broad-gauge giants with, for example, the tiny four-wheel designs of the period by Edward Bury, made them appear even bigger than they actually were. Weighing around 49 tons, they were several tons heavier than the Great Western's 'Iron Duke' Class. The 9ft-diameter drivers were flangeless and must have presented some handling and machining problems akin to those of the early Great Western orders placed by Brunel for his first loco stock. Machinery had of course improved considerably from those early times, although only about sixteen or so years before, but handling a 9ft wheel was still quite a job.

These flangeless 9ft drivers gave a speed down the Wellington Bank of about 80mph, again always commented on by railway historians, but the main question they usually fail to ask is how did the locomotives perform going up the Wellington Bank with wet rails and a full load? Of the 4-2-4 wheel arrangement, the two '4s' were swivelling bogies pivoting on ball and sockets, and the first batch of locos were braked on the trailing bogie only, but the Bristol Works replacements were braked on all wheels.

Before being taken over by the Great Western in 1876, production at the works speeded up with eight 2-4-0s between 1870 and 1872 followed by a mix of 2-4-0, 0-4-0, 0-6-0 and a solitary replacement 4-2-4 giant in 1873. Almost all were to the broad-gauge format, but a total of ten standard gauge were built, two of them completed after the Great Western takeover. With the exception of one of the big 4-2-4s, which was destroyed in an accident at Long Ashton in 1876 (caused by the state of the track), the 9ft specials were all converted to 4-2-2 tender engines the year after takeover with 8ft drivers with flanges. The rear bogie was also removed and replaced by a single pair of 4ft 6in wheels.

Up to the absorption into the GWR, the Bristol Workshops had produced thirty-five loco-motives to run on tracks built to three separate gauges, 4ft 8½in, 7ft 0¼in and the 3ft 0in gauge of the Burlescombe quarry line, or 'Westleigh Tramway', two of the total for the tramway.

Several contractors had been involved with the total stock. Of the twenty-six saddle-tank batch built between 1855 and 1873, those involved included Rothwell & Co. who built six, Beyer Peacock supplied four, there were ten more from Vulcan Foundry and a further half-dozen from the Avonside Engine Company (which recently changed its name from Stothert & Slaughter). These engines were utilised for both passenger and goods traffic, and as the broad-gauge lines of the branches were converted to narrow gauge, the batch was transferred to the South Devon and Cornwall area. The Great Western itself also supplied locomotives before the urge for independence manifested itself on the Bristol & Exeter.

An odd conversion, narrow to broad then back to narrow gauge, occurred in 1870, when five locomotives from the Worcester Engine Company went through the shops for converting for the Highbridge, Bridgwater and Yeovil traffic. Conversion back to narrow gauge occurred in 1875.

A little-known firm also supplied one engine to the Bristol & Exeter, a firm later to be auctioned bit by bit until all the contents had gone, when buildings were to be disposed of to Saxby & Farmer the signal manufacturers, itself to become part of the well-known Westinghouse Brake & Signal Company of Chippenham, Wiltshire. Rowland and Peter Brotherhood, of Railway Works, Chippenham, sold a six-coupled broad-gauge tank engine to the Bristol & Exeter in 1874. It is not really clear whether this was rebuilt from another source or a new engine and it seemed to hang around for a number of years before its purchase by the Bristol & Exeter.

The firm itself was established in 1842 to make general railway fittings, points and crossings, signal equipment and wagon components, until brother Peter branched out into steam locomotives about 1857. Around the 1869–72 period the crash came and the firm disappeared, having supplied locomotives to several railways including the Scole Railway in Norfolk and the London, Chatham & Dover Railway. In all from the Bristol & Exeter a total of ninety-five broad-gauge engines were taken over by the Great Western – twenty-eight to narrow gauge and two small ones for the 3ft-gauge tramway. Quite soon after the takeover Pearson, the loco superintendent, retired.

It has been stated before that repairing locomotives is vastly different to the job of constructing them in the first place. In the case of the big 4-2-4 tank locos, with the forerunners of the fleet built by contract, it is more than reasonable to assume that although built or assembled at Bristol a number of components were not actually made there! Any jigs, fixtures and patterns for castings, such as there would have been at that time, were already at the contractors, as well as the know-how and expertise to make a 9ft-diameter wheel. Whilst such a wheel could be turned and recontoured at the Bristol Shops, the facilities were not there to actually make one and it would make sense to purchase such an item from the contractors.

The small output from the shops made it an uneconomic proposition to install full manufacturing facilities – particularly to make – for example, three and the later one, of the big tank locos. On takeover by the Great Western, the shops were used for repairs, no more construction as such being undertaken.

Following takeover in 1876, the Great Western closed its locomotive depot at South Wales Junction. A year later, with broad gauge reducing, the Bristol Works itself was converted into a double turntable (45ft) running shed, for the 4ft 8½in gauge whilst still retaining a facility for erecting and repairs only.

Further alterations occurred at the workshops in 1892. The mixed- and broad-gauge need had by now disappeared – standard gauge was the order of the day. Due to extreme pressure on Temple Meads some form of relief or avoiding line had become essential. The proposal was for a double-track line to complete the rails triangle with the river and sweep across the Avon via a new bridge at the rear of the workshop end of the twin table shed. With any new locomotive building long since taken over by Swindon, which also took on the heavy and major repairing role, the Bristol Workshops were cut virtually in half and one bay demolished. The wall of arches that had supported the centre was partially stone blocked in and glazed. At the wide end of the wedge of land between what was now the workshop outer wall and the relief or avoiding line, a turntable was installed with access into or through the workshop via an open arch in the new wall, with a table track around the periphery of the narrow building also (see illustration plate and map). The relief lines also connected to the turntable from the narrow end of the wedge.

The dual rail complication died with the broad gauge in 1892 – the converted conglomerate of buildings surviving until 1931 and accommodating about 100 locos ranging from 0-4-0 to 4-4-0 and about twenty 4-6-0 of the 2900 Class.

This was the period of the extensive railway rebuilding programme initiated by a government desire to reduce the depression effects on employment. Analysis of the site showed a total rebuild was required, causing the old Bristol & Exeter layout to disappear, replaced by new workshops and a ten-road running shed. This new complex had a much neater appearance than the old Bristol & Exeter layout.

In another thirty-five years even steam itself had vanished and the relief line would be reduced to a single track.

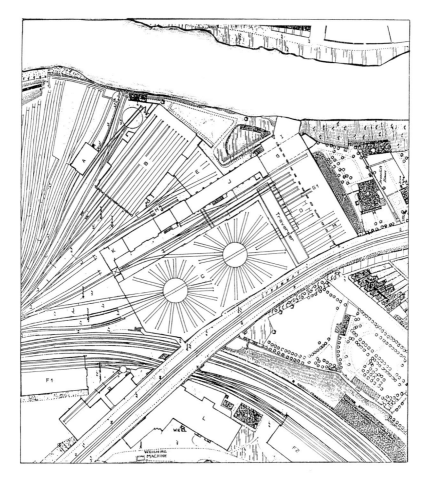

The Bristol & Exeter Railway workshops at Bristol (Bath Rd), 1884. Originally opened in around 1851, they were extended by the Bristol & Exeter in 1854 and enlarged by the Great Western after takeover in 1876. They were completely demolished, redesigned and rebuilt in 1929–34.

Key

A	Coal stage
B	Broad-gauge shed. Note mixed- & broad-gauged track.
C	Standard-gauge running shed of 1877 with two 45ft turntables.
D	Workshop. Note that there are four rails instead of the usual three for mixed track. It ensured that the inspection pits were central under both broad- and standard-gauge locomotives.
E	Broad-gauge carriage shop
F1, F2	Goods sheds – inward & outward goods
G1	Fitting & heavy machine shop
G	Fitting & machine shop
H	Weighbridge
I	Smiths' shop
J	Carpenters' shop
K	Offices
L	Original broad-gauge workshops (1851)

The 1892 Bristol avoiding line entailed demolition of half of the workshop building. Part of Sections I, and G, all of G1 and M were levelled.

Outside the late Bristol & Exeter sheds at Bristol after takeover by the Great Western, *c.* 1885 stands a Pearson 4-2-4 tank engine converted by the GWR into a tender 4-2-2. The clock building survived the alterations of the mid-1920s until its final demise in 1932.

Bristol & Exeter Railway: Pearson tank driving wheels of 9ft diameter, preserved at York Railway Museum.

Sheds & workshops of the Bristol & Exeter Railway.

Viewed from a passing train (1923), on the left can be seen the coal stage. The two centre buildings are the broad-gauge running sheds demolished around 1932. Extreme right are the offices and workshops; behind, narrow-gauge sheds.

Continuing from the right of the photo above (c. 1926). The standard-gauge running sheds of 1877, ex-workshop and erecting bays to rear. Note alteration to extreme left-hand building compared to the 1923 photograph.

The empty works in around 1926 prior to its complete demolition and rebuilding in 1932. Note the Bristol avoiding line (at the bottom of the photograph), the construction of which in 1892 meant the demolition and clearance of half of the workshop, the inner supporting pillars now forming the outer wall. (See also site plan of 1884, p.85).

The now single avoiding line on the right with the turntable. Note the low angled brick and stone wall base behind the turntable. This image shows part of the original works prior to the alterations of 1892.

Construction of the new running sheds. Note back right the (broad-gauge) running sheds and at the top right corner of the new sheds the remaining portion of the old office block. The section of wall in the foreground is the old external wall (originally the centre division before 1892) of the workshops.

The new lifting shop being completed on the site of the old broad-gauge running sheds. The new coal stage is also nearing completion. On the left are the new running sheds.

The new lifting shop completed (1934) and still in pristine condition.

The workshops and depot at Bristol, Bath Road, c. 1992. The only reminder of old Bristol & Exeter steam days is the length of wall adjacent the road on the left of this composite photograph.

A further reminder of Bristol and Exeter steam: a locomotive and stalwart railway staff photographed in 1848 at Tiverton.

3

Monmouthshire Railway & Canal Company

Bolt Street (Later Dock Street) Works, Newport

This company had a very early start to its dual-function life, beginning with the boom for canals, which, in the canal world, was akin to the locomotive boom of forty years later. The Monmouthshire Canal was approved in 1792, in company with a number of others during the same period. It ran from Pontnewynydd to the River Usk at Newport with a branch to Crumlin Bridge. Included in the Act was permission to include a railway or tramway to adjacent iron works, quarries and coal mines. Thus the canal company was already in the tramway business from the start. The horse was the tractive power and operations commenced in 1799.

Later in this book is a note on the Tredegar Iron Works of Mr Sam Homphray and it is due to him that the first whiff of steam was smelled on the Monmouthshire system. In 1829, he purchased a locomotive from Robert Stephenson & Company and decided on what would now be called an 'Away Day' by taking a trip along the adjacent and linking tramroad tracks. A plodding horse and a small loaded truck are a vastly different proposition to a steam locomotive, even though it was a small one of less than 9 tons. Setting off on his own 'cheap day return' excursion, the overenthusiastic Sam spent most of it repairing the track torn up and damaged by his engine, just about making the 20 miles to Bassaleg after numerous derailments.

Repairs to the track and getting his engine back on the rails were only some of his day's worries. On a reasonable stretch of the metals, with things seemingly very good at last and the urge to speed up irresistible, a low tree branch neatly took off the chimney and that was the end of that for the day at least! One thing the journey proved was that something more substantial than the usual plate or early edge rails track would be needed for a steam locomotive. Several months later, with the track well strengthened and the locomotive behaving itself very well, a routine steam journey was commenced for real. Everyday an amount of coal averaging about 55 tons was hauled down from the collieries at two-thirds the cost of horse transport, the 28-mile trip certainly paying for itself handsomely.

With a good mix of canals, railroads and the crude tramroad, the company had a monopoly of the local transport and this did not please many of their customers. There were always complaints concerning costs of freighting and condition of the track and facilities, which included a passenger service of a sorts. An updating was essential, and in 1845 the Newport and Pontypool Act started the general facelift into a proper 4ft 8½in-gauge railway, but the updating, particularly on the plate tramways, was a massive task.

A slumbering progress was awakened by the hiss of the new steam engines, which were sounding warnings to all of the country's canals that a real opposition had arrived. With an eye to the future, the joint company started its main steam railway operations a number of years after the railway boom had settled somewhat and it had become obvious that the locomotive was here to stay, to the detriment of canals.

Orders were placed with various firms for the first batch of engines, the Neath Abbey Iron Company receiving an order for four in 1848. These 0-6-0s were to the standard gauge of 4ft 8½in with 15 × 24in cylinders and 4ft-diameter wheels. A year earlier an 0-8-0 had been ordered from Grylls & Co. of Llanelly, but with square 16 × 16in cylinders it was not a success and within two years was on the sale list. The firm itself was a bit of a mystery regarding financing and organisation, and in 1848 went bankrupt. It had made locomotives for several companies but of the few made none was really successful.

The other maker was Stothert & Slaughter, supplying 0-6-0s, but records are scanty on this score so no details are known. Whatever the locos were, and they were certainly heavier than Sam Homphray's, problems arose again when the line opened in 1849 as they were all too heavy for the track. After a hurried appraisal, horse power was substituted for the steam locos to keep some sort of traffic running and an intense track relaying programme instituted once more.

The requirements of updating from an original pioneering tramway to an up-to-date railway contained all sorts of problems. An update of the track was a top priority but first a compromise was required. A 'bridge' rail was introduced, which had an extended inner flange. The bridge rail was at 4ft 8½in gauge, and the extended inner flange allowed continued use of the plateway tracks, which had a rail gauge (wheels not flanged) of 4ft 4in. The wheel problem affected the locomotives as well, of course, and they required a rebuild to cover the introduction of flanged wheels and wider gauge. Conversion of tracks and locomotives continued apace and held the stage in the interim, until new tracks and more updated locomotives could be introduced to a uniform rail network system.

A few plateways and tramroads associated with the Monmouthshire Railway could not be converted because of location and terrain problems of very sharp curves and steep slopes.

These remained in their pioneer forms until eventual closure, when the area was worked out or some other fate befell the reason for their existence.

William Craig, the loco superintendent, thus had quite a job integrating not only the track problems but the conversion or acquisition of existing and new locomotives respectively to suit the track. The maintenance of locomotives had not been neglected and by 1854, when he resigned to take a similar (if possibly less stressful) job on the Manchester, Sheffield & Lincolnshire Railway, he had a fully equipped Repair Shop and Depot at Crumlin and another Depot under way at Pill. The locomotives in his charge, twenty-five of them, were in the process of conversion to standard gauge during overhaul with new up-to-date locomotives on order. He left with the satisfaction of a job well done and a very profitable company going from strength to strength.

A new superintendent, Richard Laybourne, arrived in 1854 from the London North Western Railway. His struggles with his locomotives and track coincided with British struggles against the Russians as the war in the Crimea continued. He was quickly into the fray of organisation, and a repair and building shop was ordered and constructed as the Bolt Street Works, Newport.

The stock conversions required were completed quite early in Laybourne's tenure of office; carriages, wagons and locomotives were now modernised. However, not all of them were updated to the new look. Three locos were retained in tramway condition, along with other suitable stock, for use on those lines that had retained horse power but had fallen foul of a ban on the use of such traction. The section of the Monmouthshire that included the Rumney Railway was a case in point. A further problem was the second relaying of track from the combination rail mentioned previously to the 'edge' rail proper. This entailed a major interruption and a reduction in services for a period. Further jobs undertaken by Laybourne in his update programme were the implications of a change of fuel from coke to coal, and the rebuild of locomotive fireboxes to suit. With all this work it is not surprising that it was not until 1867 that the first new loco, an 0-6-0 saddle tank, emerged from the shops, and although built as new, it was not strictly actually made there. The works was quite small and the facilities limited, so many components were supplied by contract from outside and assembled at Bolt Street.

Trade at the docks continued to increase from the opening in 1849 when hundreds of tons of tramplates and sleepers had been required to extend siding accommodation to docks that were becoming crammed to capacity. The facilities for locomotive and stock maintenance were also becoming inadequate, and finalising the Bolt Street Works in 1857 included the demolition of earlier facilities at Court-y-Bella and Crumlin and using the timber and stone to add carriage and wagon repair shops at Bolt Street.

Between 1867, when locomotive building commenced, and 1875, when the company was absorbed by the Great Western, a total of nine locomotives were built. The wheel format was the usual 0-6-0 with four to an 4-4-0 design, the latter quite rare outside the London area as they were side tanks with outside cylinders. Cylinder size for all was the same 16 × 24in, probably to fit in with the existing machinery to finish bore and valve faces and as an attempt at standardisation of components for ease of maintenance.

This latter attempt was a half-hearted affair, really, as dimensions varied between locos of the same design. The boilers in particular varied: a few inches here and there did not seem to concern anyone, as long as the construction was properly done. With a building policy of one or two locos per year and the rest of any batch purchased from outside, along with major components, the whole building commitment was a rather leisurely affair.

There is bound to be a financial crisis in any company and one hit the Monmouthshire in the 1850s from a rather indirect source. This had nothing really to do with railway matters as such, but with the technological introduction in the decade of a steel-making process, the Bessemer method. A quicker, cheaper way of producing a replacement material for puddle wrought iron sorted the wheat from the chaff in the works of the producers. Those who didn't (wouldn't or couldn't) modernise went out of business, and competition became cut-throat; but eventually, after economies, the problem eased.

In 1868, when Richard Laybourne resigned for fresh challenges as manager of the Rhymney Iron Company, he bequeathed thirty-eight locomotives and associated updated stock to his successor.

A new superintendent, Henry Appleby (late of the West Cornwall Railway), had taken over in 1868 and he had a dual role in that he was a sort of adviser or consultant also to the Neath & Brecon Railway, which, presumably on his advice, purchased 4-4-0s from contractors to virtually the same design as those of the Monmouthshire Railway & Canal Company's own. It is interesting to note that Appleby's predecessor had been among the first railway engineers, in about 1855, to use cast-iron brake blocks in place of the hardwood baulks usually used at that time.

Appleby attempted to standardise designs to a certain extent and his 0-4-4 side tanks and eight freight traffic 0-6-0 saddle tanks were a step in this direction. When Swindon took control in 1875, two side-tank designs were in the early stages of completion and were soon whipped away to be finished at the main works. The 0-6-0 side tanks were also given the 'Swindon treatment', being converted to 0-4-4s, as were the remaining six of the batch that had been completed by contractors.

With the company came its stock of fifty-three locomotives, all of course to the 4ft 8½in gauge, and the end of building at Bolt Street. Running and light repairs only were to continue; all rebuilding or heavy repairs would be channelled to Swindon or Wolverhampton Works.

It is a strange coincidence that the last steam locomotive to survive from the Monmouthshire Railway fleet, No. 1346, was sold through an intermediary in 1910 to the Tredegar Iron Works, where it survived until 1928. In this way the last of the steam locomotives was owned by the company that had introduced steam to the Monmouthshire in the first place almost a century before.

From drawings available it would appear that the Bolt Street Works, once established in the 1850s, altered very little over the years up to its partial demolition in 1918. Whilst its function updated as locomotives developed, the buildings remained almost untouched.

The Bolt Street Works, as constructed in 1854 had the look of a Bourne print about it. The Bourne print of the erecting shop at Swindon showing the very deep traverser pit could have been sketched at Bolt Street, which covered an area of about 160ft × 143ft, with pit roads off either side of the track. Having been a repair depot for thirty or so years, and looking rather decrepit as well as having certain inconveniences, Bolt Street was demolished during the First World War.

During 1918 the breakers moved in and some of the site was cleared, a new but smaller complex replacing the old shops and offices. Rising from the rubble was a Churchward standard shed, which opened in 1920. It had a very short steam life, closing in 1929. Now known as Dock Street, the last years were spent catering for wagon repairs until it was closed in 1963. A portion of the old Bolt Street Works is now used by a timber merchant.

Opposite top: Newport (Bolt Street) workshops *c.* 1862. (Late Monmouthsire Railway & Canal Co. GWR from 1880)

Opposite bottom: Newport (Bolt Street) workshops on closure, *c.* 1918. (Late Monmouthsire Railway & Canal Co. GWR from 1880)

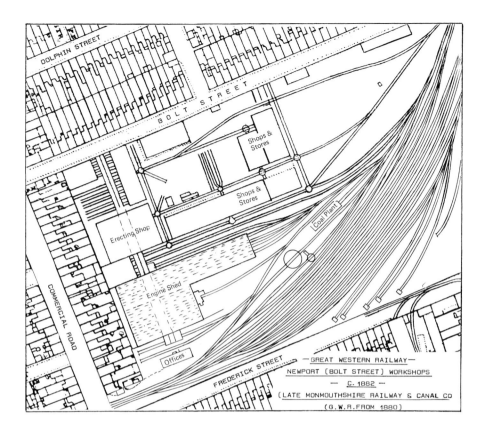

DOLPHIN STREET

BOLT STREET

Shops & Stores

Shops & Stores

Coal Plant

Erecting Shop

COMMERCIAL ROAD

Engine Shed

Offices

FREDERICK STREET

—GREAT WESTERN RAILWAY—
NEWPORT (BOLT STREET) WORKSHOPS
— C. 1882 —
(LATE MONMOUTHSHIRE RAILWAY & CANAL C.º
(G.W.R.FROM 1880)

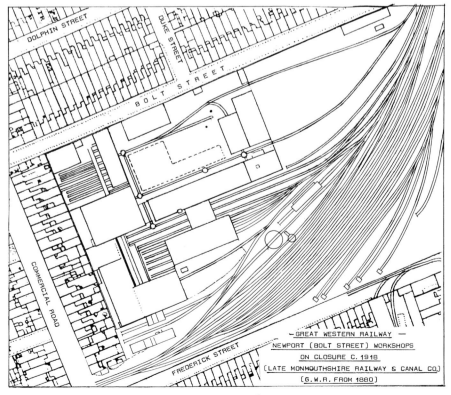

DOLPHIN STREET

DUKE STREET

BOLT STREET

COMMERCIAL ROAD

FREDERICK STREET

—GREAT WESTERN RAILWAY —
NEWPORT (BOLT STREET) WORKSHOPS
ON CLOSURE C. 1918
(LATE MONMOUTHSHIRE RAILWAY & CANAL CO.)
(G.W.R. FROM 1880)

Bolt Street workshops just prior to demolition.

The 1840s workshop at Swindon. The old-type deep traverser pits are a main feature.

4

Cambrian Railway Works, Oswestry, 1865

The combining of several smaller companies in 1864–65 formed the nucleus of the Cambrian Railwa, and the various locomotives involved in forming the new company now required a maintenance base. The board decided that a knowledgeable outside firm should be consulted in this matter and who better than a firm which dealt in railway motive power itself? An approach was made to Sharp Stewart & Company of Manchester and, with an idea of the Cambrian requirements, a design for a workshop was produced. The engineering works were transferred from Welshpool to Oswestry in 1866 with Mr Alexander Walker as the first Locomotive Superintendent. The total mileage of the Cambrian was now 170 miles.

The new shop was rectangular, with massive supporting stone columns separating the structure into three along its length. It was a traverser shop design in which the central bay contained a traversing table, which in turn served eleven pit roads on either side – one bay of eleven pits being for erecting work and the opposite bay for boiler repairs. Several pits in the boiler bay were reserved for tender maintenance, the boiler and riveting facilities being available for the necessary plate work on the tenders.

The shop was built in 1865 from the Sharp Stewart designs by Thomas Savin & Company, and much of the machinery installed had also been supplied by the designers of the shop. In this latter event it would be possible, with cost saving in mind and with possible Cambrian approval, to get rid of some of the older machinery on a second-hand basis, and as Sharp Stewart is recorded as having supplied machinery, this could have happened. A wheel lathe, say, which is still serviceable, but with larger locomotive development possibly a little small for Sharp Stewart requirements, could certainly be unloaded onto the Cambrian which had no major express passenger locomotives of the size of those running on the major companies' metals. Sharp Stewart were, of course, also machine manufacturers in their own right so certainly they would also benefit from the order by selling new machinery. Their output included all of the main requirements of lathes, drilling machines, and planing, punching and shearing machines – all-in-all, a very lucrative order. In addition they could supply ferrous and non-ferrous castings for general or locomotive use.

The shops were used for the general maintenance of the stock, which had been supplied by contract. The shop layout itself would have been suitable for locomotive building, but the supporting facilities, whilst adequate for maintenance, were not really up to the actual making of components. The only 'building' that took place was the assembly of two of the 4-4-0 passenger 61 Class, over the period 1901–04. These locos were to the design of Sharp Stewart, who had built or were building twenty of a batch of twenty-two. Many of the components, including complete boilers, came from outside; the boilers used for the two home-constructed locos were actually spares for the class and supplied by Nasmyth Wilson several years before. Other items came from Robert Stephenson, so again a very mixed effort from several sources went into the construction programme.

New tenders were constructed at the works, but only several years after the locos had been running – up until then using a pair of spare tenders in stock for the batch. Nothing more in the new sense was built and the two locos in question ran until the reappraisal of stock which came with the amalgamations of 1921. Two or three years later they were scrapped; one had been placed for sale, but no one was interested in purchase.

On amalgamation the old Cambrian Workshops were subjected to review, in company with others, and several proposals for alteration were prepared. Among the facilities that would go was the small brass foundry. Brass components, as far as possible, would now be Great Western, produced complete at Swindon Works. Repositioning the sawmill and carpenters' shop also saw various proposals, the latter ending in the sheet house, no longer required with supplies available from Great Western sources.

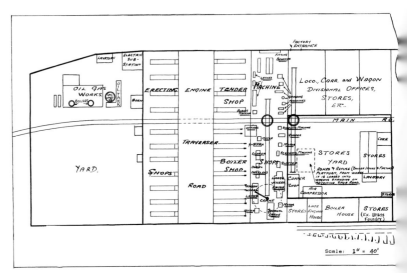

GWR Locomotive, Carriage & Wagon Works, Oswestry (1937). Originally the workshops of the Cambrian Railway.

Scale: 1" = 40'

The general pattern of repairs continued with the locos of the Cambrian area, but with the end of steam in sight during the 1950s there was an overall air of running down.

To the works at Oswestry must go the award for being the last GWR and almost the last British Rail (BR) works to repair official steam. Whilst main works were, during the 1960s, anticipating the transition to diesel, steam locomotives were farmed out in their twilight years, with some unusual and mixed bags of stock appearing for repair. The last locomotive was a standard, in for a re-tubing job, No. 75024, virtually new but destined to be scrapped in November 1967 when only 14 years old.

Amongst the locos dealt with were 'decapods', the 92000 Class 2-10-0s some of the largest existing on BR as it was, several Class 5s from the London Midland and Scottish Railway, and a mix of GWR classes from the 9400 pannier tanks to 'Castles' and 'Counties'. All-in-all it was certainly out of the normal run of things compared with the former classes that worked over the Cambrian section.

The locomotive works effectively closed with the last steam repair completed on 31 December 1966, outliving the carriage & wagon works by about two and half years. The carriage & wagon works remained in engineering, being taken over by the well-known engineers Davis & Metcalf, makers of injectors for the steamers now passing into history. Not all steam had vanished, however, as Oswestry had been responsible for the maintenance of the narrow(er) gauge (1ft 11in) Vale of Rheidol locomotives which were forwarded to Derby Works along with responsibility of maintenance.

By the time of closure, the staff had reduced to about forty, with a number approaching retirement age. Some craftsmen were re-employed by Davis & Metcalfe, and whilst the older staff would find re-employment difficult, the oldest man on the payroll, a 67-year-old coppersmith, was in some demand due to the very nature of his craft skill, not now required for the steam locomotives on which it had been so long practised.

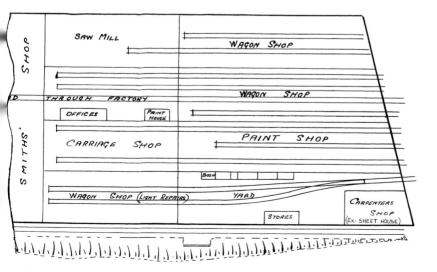

Above and below: The erecting bay at Oswestry, *c.* 1925 (photograph taken from the crane).
Note the massive construction of the walls and the supporting buttress of the crane rails.

The brass foundry in the 1920s.

5

Caerphilly Works

Expansion of facilities was not of course confined solely to the Great Western, and many companies developed and applied their own expansion plans as traffic increased.

The intention of Rhymney Railway was to connect from its initial Rhymney–Hengoed line to the docks at Cardiff. Following friction with the Taff Vale Company over the routing, the Rhymney Railway decided to go it alone via a specially constructed tunnel. The Rhymney were bailed out of this rather rash and costly exercise, no matter how necessary they felt it to be, by the London North Western.

The London North Western Railway was also spreading in the area, and the financial difficulties that the Rhymney experienced in 1866, within a decade of its inception, gave the London North Western a foot in the door with access to the docks as the prize. The bail bond entailed taking over, on paper, all of the Rhymney's rolling stock, which carried on running as before and continued to be maintained at Cardiff Docks, at the works established near the running sheds. Each loco carried a little brass plate, which detailed the names of the nominal new owners.

Whilst adequate at the beginning, the growth in the area in the early 1870s and 1880s with more stock in use and expansion continuing meant that a larger works would very rapidly be essential. Land was at a premium in the docks area, so a look elsewhere was necessary. An area of about 17 acres at Caerphilly was purchased just before the turn of the century. On this land was built the new works; to the west end of the long site were the carriage & wagon shops, and to the east the locomotive section.

Initially to be an addition to the Cardiff facilities, with both operating together, it was decided early on that Caerphilly would be the main and only works. The design for the locomotive shop was for one large, subdivided building about 280ft wide and 250ft long. The carriage & wagon shop, also a single subdivided building being about 220ft and 12ft wide.

The loco shop had six sub divisions, which comprised machine, boiler, erecting and smith shops and two designated test shops. One of these, nominally the boiler test shop, also contained metal stores and for a period the tool room, and the second contained within its 35ft width, brake and component testing as well as being home to the weigh bridge equipment. The 'bosh' or component cleaning facilities were in this shop and at the east end was an area reserved for the coppersmiths' section.

For materials handling cranes were installed: two 30-ton cranes over the longitudinal bays for the erecting shop, a 'walking crane' in the machine shop, and a 10-tonner over the boiler bays. The erecting shop followed the layout of many of the steam loco shops with the notable exception of Swindon, in that the locomotives were dealt with in line, the rail tracks running the length of the shop. The boiler bay was also an in-line layout. This was in effect a space-saving layout, as with separate cross tracks a large area had to be set aside for the traversing table necessary to move locos about within the shop, or in and out of the shop, dependent on crane facilities and use of the shop itself. Everything in a 'lengthwise' shop had to be lifted over everything else or moved forward as repairs or construction progressed. Pits were positioned between the long tracks, bridged by movable plates as required.

Standardisation was not the prerogative of the Great Western where loco components were concerned. The Rhymney Railway management introduced a programme at this time for as much standardisation as possible with a scrapping programme for those locos that could not be easily included in the programme. Around 1906 a standard boiler was designed, along with cylinder castings that could be fitted to the range of tank engines that comprised the stock majority, there being fewer tender locomotive types. With the exception of four previously withdrawn the locomotive stock at this period included the company's original engines.

Retaining side-tank design and the tried-and-trusted 0-6-2 wheel arrangement used extensively in the Welsh mining areas, Robert Stephenson had the contract for replacement engines as some of the originals were at the end of their active life. Also at this time, many companies were dabbling in the 'rail car' concept, a coach or coaches combined with a steam traction unit. For branch work these were proving an interesting combination without using or requiring the separate train layout of an engine and a coach – the loco being overpower when pulling a single coach, thus wasting capacity. The Rhymney decided to obtain two of the car units.

These were contracted to Hudswell Clarke, the works itself without the capacity to build locomotives from scratch, although heavy repairs and rebuilding of the normal locomotives were undertaken without problems. Following the First World War, when items were again subject to more close scrutiny and much needed overhauls, more new locos were obtained from the usual contractors and hiring of locos from the Great Western and Great Central Railways occurred – such was the demand.

The proposed standardisation of pre-war years was recommended after the war but was to be short-lived, brought to a halt by the Railway Grouping Act of 1921. The Rhymney and its adjacent fellows were about to lose their identities and the Great Western was due to expand once again.

A full detail of all stock and buildings possessed by the lines concerned was forwarded to the Great Western at Swindon and intensive inspections instigated. The Rhymney stock was found to be generally well maintained – but of course all of the stock so absorbed was now subject to the Great Western's own standardisation ideas, to start with the renumbering to suit Great Western practice. Later would follow the use of the distinctive Great Western style boilers and fittings.

Caerphilly, once solely for Rhymney engines, soon began to take stock from adjacent absorbed lines some en route to Swindon after initial examination – never to return and condemned outright on arrival. A scheme for enlarging the facilities at Caerphilly was proposed and then shelved in 1923, several adjacent companies also toying with expansion proposals for existing facilities, which came to nought due to the Act of 1921.

Adjacent Barry was a candidate for a proposed major works status, but as the work built up the problem earlier experienced at Wolverhampton raised its head. A works that required expansion had to have space in which to do just that, and in many potential expansion areas the ground available was either not big enough or just did not exist. (See p.152 for Layout Plan of Barry Works.)

The centralisation of repairs of locomotives, not only those of the absorbed companies but of Great Western stock allocated to the area, meant that a major works was urgently required. Space was available at Caerphilly and so the dice was cast. Caerphilly would be expanded. The Great Western was very fortunate to have really an ideal site on a plate.

Situated where it was, not hemmed in by any industrial developments, the site was ideal for expansion actually internally. The rectangular site, with its loco shops at one end and carriage and wagon facilities at the other, had a large empty centre section (apart from railway access lines), and this was where the new locomotive shop was to be built. The new shop was again to be a single building, but to the design of the A shop at Swindon – short pit lines at 90° to a central traversing table road, within an approximate 300 × 200ft area. With two repair bays of seventeen pits each and overhead an 80-ton crane above each pit, the shop was very spacious for the nature and type of repair expected, nominally the tank engines of the area only. Capacity on each pit allowed two tank-type engines to be worked at at the same time, so in total a figure of around sixty locomotives could be accommodated at any one time, although in practice this was not intended. A quick look at a photograph of this shop shows how closely it resembles the A shop at Swindon, and for which it could be mistaken, the A shop already expanded a decade earlier.

At Caerphilly, with the new shop operating by 1928, the original shops were redesignated. The old erecting shop became the new boiler shop and the old boiler shop was refurbished with a new floor and machinery to become the wheel shop. The machine shop was retained and equipped with some new machinery to become the heavy machine shop. The test shop, again re-equipped, became a light machine shop. The boiler test shop was split into a spring shop with all the usual equipment, and a coppersmiths' shop. Least affected of all was the smiths' shop, which continued as before but with a few new items of equipment, among them being a 15cwt steam hammer.

At this time the carriage and wagon side of the works fell right out of favour. Work diminished and laying-off of staff occurred. It was ten years before recovery was felt, and a rebirth of the carriage repair programme heralded a new carriage repair shop just prior to the outbreak of the Second World War. The new shops were approximately 420ft by 72ft.

The 1927 reorganisation and new building programme at Caerphilly also introduced a rethink of the method and sequence of locomotive repairs. In May 1929, a new circuit idea was instituted for repairs, replacing the previous method in which one gang took a locomotive from 'stripping to steaming' condition without moving from the pit over which it was positioned on entry to the shop for repair.

At Swindon, frame alignment was being aided in the early 1930s by an optical apparatus from Karl Ziess of Germany, and this also heralded a rethink of repair methods. This led to the much vaunted 'circuit' system of repair introduced around 1933. Caerphilly had beaten them to it five years before, but the question of who copied whom is never mentioned with reference to Swindon! In both places the output of repaired locomotives increased considerably and the system was retained until the end of steam.

Various machinery and lifting items at Caerphilly were updated over the years following the general depression years of the early 1930s, years which had their effect throughout the world. Recovery was finally beginning when the Second World War occurred. Immediately after the conflict a major change occurred that affected all the railway systems. 'Nationalisation' reared its ugly head and Great Western influence diminished under a standardisation blanket, muffled in terms of British Railways (Western Region).

Having been nominally a tank-engine repair factory, Caerphilly had a rebirth of fame in the 1950s, possibly assisted by the reorganisation of the nationalisation requirements. A flow

Workshops of the Rhymney Railway prior to the development at Caerphilly with the floor looking well worn!

of large tender engines appeared for repair. Whilst a visit from Their Majesties the 'Kings' did not occur, most of the other large Great Western tender classes were represented in the shops. The flow started on a smaller basis with 2-6-0s of 53XX and 63XX Classes, followed by Halls & Granges and a County 4-6-0 1000 Class. In 1957 a 2-6-2T Class 3 paid a visit and was followed by a fleeting visit by a Castle which apparently belonged to Weight Watchers – as it was weighed and quickly departed, no doubt satisfied with the figures!

Two very contrasting engines appeared in the late 1950s: *City of Truro* which had been refurbished quite recently from York Museum but had argued with a coal stage, damaging its cab, and later a 'decapped' (2-10-0) Class 9, a product of nationalisation and looking nothing like its Great Western associates. The flow continued and whilst very welcome with Castles, Austerities, a London Midland Tank 2-6-4, Halls, Counties and 0-6-0s coming in, there was an air of something ominous about it all. Were they coming to Caerphilly because something was occurring where they were normally dealt with?

Conversion of shops for diesel repairs was commenced and, although the flow of steam locos continued, the carriage shops closed in 1962. Steam loco repairs soon changed to locos being sent in for scrapping! The year 1963 started with a shop full of steam locos under repair or for cutting up. As the shop emptied, so it remained empty. A 'Hall' came in for weighing only, amid a diminishing number of staff engaged on machinery removal from the dying works. Soon only one loco remained.

In April 1963, No. 5203, a 2-6-2 tank, was taken on the traversing table out of the erecting shop. Last one out switch off the light and close the door!

The Caerphilly site is now an industrial estate.

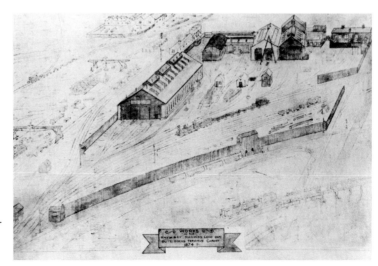

The Bute Docks terminus of the Rhymney Railway, Cardiff. A sketch drawn in 1874!

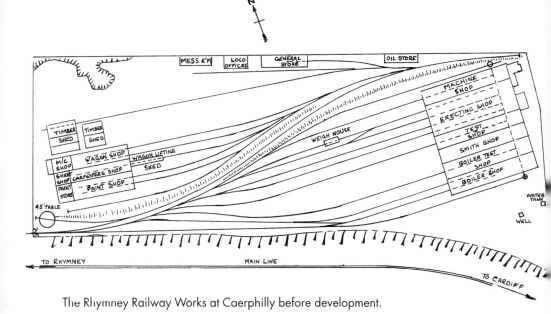

The Rhymney Railway Works at Caerphilly before development.

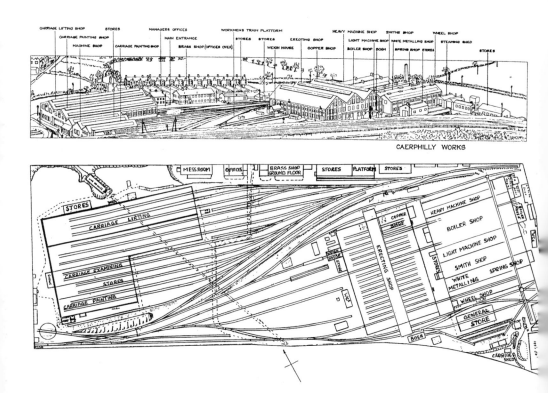

CAERPHILLY WORKS

Caerphilly Works (Ex Rhymney Railway) as redeveloped during the 1920s.

The erecting shop in the early days became the boiler shop during the 1920s.

Caerphilly Works: inside the erecting shop.

Caerphilly Works: engine erecting shop (continued from right of previous photograph).

Exterior view of the locomotive works, Caerphilly.

Traversing table in the locomotive erecting shop, Caerphilly.

The boiler shop at Caerphilly Works.

Smiths' shop at Caerphilly. Remained as a smiths' shop in the 1920 reorganisation.

The coppersmiths' shop at Caerphilly.

6

Newton Abbot Works – South Devon Railway, Absorbed by GWR in 1876

A Bill passed by Parliament in 1844 introduced the Plymouth, Devonport & Exeter Railway, a line with backing from three companies already established in the railway world. The 51½ miles of track were to be to the 7ft gauge of the backing companies, the Great Western, Bristol & Exeter, and Bristol & Gloucester railways, but there were certain initial differences in the new company which would certainly distinguish it from its founders. Its name would be changed to South Devon Railway, but the most outstanding feature would be decided at its first directors' meeting. The persuasive arguments put forward by Brunel would introduce Samunda's Atmospheric System to a full-scale railway application – a very unfortunate association with a system that, while theoretically excellent and cheap, came to be viewed as the 'atmospheric debacle' and one too well known to repeat again here. Suffice to say that from a general meeting held on 28 August 1848 to discuss the future of the system, the report concluded:

The cost of working the Atmospheric system ... so much greater than your Directors had reason to anticipate ... After most earnestly balancing the various circumstances ... have arrived at the conclusion, with the entire concurrence and on the recommendation of Mr Brunel, that it is expedient for them to suspend the use of the Atmospheric system until the same shall be made efficient at the expense of the Patentees and Mr Samunda.

The Board are prepared with arrangements for supplying locomotive power from the date of suspension of the Atmospheric System.

Experiments continued but, beaten by the technology of the period, the system died and its assets were sold off.

The legacy of the experiment (for that is all it really was), was a single line, sharply curved, steep gradient, 40-mile track layout and a company with no money left!

Brunel retained his position (possibly any other person would have been dismissed) and various changes in the board occurred. A massive majority vote for complete abandonment of the Atmospheric was taken. Directors were reduced from 21 to 11. The Great Western, Bristol & Exeter, and Midland (the latter taking over from the Bristol & Gloucester Railway) were still represented on the board. From 9 September 1847, steam locomotives had been the motive power source as the Atmospheric died.

A branch line of 5 miles from Newton to Torquay was opened and motive power supplied in the form of 2-4-0s by the Great Western. An additional running shed was located at Newton for the stock so that there were now three service stations for locomotives at Newton. Costs charged for these locomotives were heavy, considering also that there was really no suitable locomotive design for hauling stock to run on a track that had such curves and gradients.

The problem was alleviated by a Gooch design of saddle tank, the first pair named *Corsair* and *Brigand*, 4-4-0s with a leading bogie. These were built at Swindon and proved a great success. Whilst the locomotives were successful, the association with the Great Western was not particularly so, and on the turn of the half-century a proposal submitted by Brunel was accepted by the directors for a contractor to run the locomotives and supply additional stock to a similar design for a period of ten years. At the end of the agreement, the South Devon was able to purchase the locomotives and stock subject to a financial adjustment in price to cover depreciation.

Part of this deal was that the contractor could use the company's maintenance shops and thus the responsibility for maintenance of the static pumping engines, never very efficient even at the best of times, had changed to maintenance of locomotive stock and the Atmospheric operators were dismissed.

From the assorted miscellany of Atmospheric leftovers had emerged a steam railway. Part of the Atmospheric rolling stock, the piston drawn carriages were converted into brake vans for the new venture into conventional railway operations. For the 58 miles of track, twelve bogie saddle tanks were at work by 1854 and were followed by four six-coupled goods engines. These were all contract built by established firms, the four contractors being Haigh Foundry, Stothart & Slaughter, Longridge & Company and Fairbairn & Son for the four-coupled bogie designs, with Vulcan Foundry supplying the six-coupled saddle tanks. During 1859–60 another dozen bogie saddle tanks were built to slightly amended dimensions by Stothart & Slaughter, becoming the 'Hawk' Class, and following the 'Comet' Class of the former batch. These engines had been designed and construction supervised by Daniel Gooch who seems to have had not only fingers in the contract pie of Geach, the contracting company, but a whole hand!

On the expiry of the contract, during which the contractor Charles Geach had died, the renewal for seven years was contracted to 'Edward Evans, Thomas Walker of Wednesbury,

Ironmaster and Daniel Gooch of Paddington, Gentlemen'. On the expiry of this second contract, when the directors resumed full control and purchased the stock as per the contract agreement, the books showed that the mileage cost charged had given a profit approaching 50 per cent – very good business for those involved!

Around the mid 1850s the Gooch family was represented at Newton Workshops by William Frederick, Daniel's younger brother who was the superintendent until 1857. He was then succeeded by John Wright who remained with the South Devon until the Great Western takeover in 1876, when he retired. A young man who had been a pupil of John Wright was transferred to Swindon from the Newton Abbot shops when his chief retired. The young man was to make his name at Swindon in later years, but for George Jackson Churchward his foot was already on the success ladder, its top already pointing in a new direction.

On the leasing of the Cornwall Railway in 1869 (by the Great Western, South Devon & Bristol & Exeter Railways), it was decided to concentrate loco servicing and repair at the Newton Abbot Works. The buildings were enlarged and 150 new houses built nearby. The station was also rebuilt around 1860 as a two-sided junction station.

Ten years before takeover, the expiry of the second contract had given the South Devon control of forty engines and also, by agreement, the control of the working of the Cornwall and the West Cornwall Railways, the latter a narrow-gauge line now committed to broad-gauge working. The shops at this time had to deal with a motley collection of engines swept up from various corners of acquisition. The smallest of these was from the Sutton Harbour Branch, where it had been introduced to replace horses. It was itself not much bigger than one of the animals it replaced, but it was broad gauge and it was a steam loco of sorts. Built by Sara & Company of Plymouth in 1868 it was an 0-4-0 with a vertical boiler, 9in × 12in cylinders and 3ft-diameter wheels. Known as 'Tiny' or 'The Coffee Pot' it chugged resolutely around the Newton Abbot yards for about twenty years when it was taken inside the workshops to be used to power machinery as a stationary engine. It kept the wheels of industry turning for forty-four years in this capacity, after which time (on electrification of the shops) it was restored as a loco for display purposes only on the station platform. It is the sole survivor of broad-gauge motive power and is now preserved.

Narrow-gauge engines from the West Cornwall Railway were exchanged for broad-gauge locos from the Llynvi and Ogmore tracks, both railways changing gauges at this time. Other contract locomotives were acquired to build up the South Devon stock and the Newton Works was kept busy on conversions of those designed to the familiar saddle-tank patterns of the South Devon.

The locomotives being dealt with during the early 1870s were still a very varied bunch. The contributions from an equally varied bunch of contractors included *King* (a 2-4-0 well tank with minuscule 9in × 16in cylinders), originally built by the Avonside Company for the Torbay & Brixham Railway, which embarrassingly the company could not find the money to pay for when the bill was presented.

The conversions included the not insignificant work of alteration not only by the addition of saddle tanks but of expanding from narrow to broad gauge. During the couple of years up to the Great Western takeover in 1876, the South Devon Locomotive Superintendent at Newton Abbot had the responsibility of running three groups as one: the South Devon, the Cornwall Joint and the West Cornwall. With the takeover came eighty-five locomotives, the Great Western then renumbered the lot (2096–2180). Some of the named engines duplicated the names of existing Great Western stock.

With the takeover came a review of the workshops. Plans were drawn up for a complete rehash which, whilst it did not occur immediately, had certainly been brought into effect by 1893.

The workshop of the old South Devon Railway had been converted or adapted into the locomotive running shed, by replacing the traversing table at the other end of the complex. At this time of course the broad-gauge requirements had gone. Up to 1924 the works could handle most of the required but limited repairs to the loco stock of the smaller natures, limited again by the 25-ton capacity of the overhead cranes in the erecting shop.

An extension to the erecting shop at this time gave not only the added capacity of more inspection pits but an increased crane capacity of 35 tons, enabling the heavier locomotives to be lifted – albeit single ended – for attention to all wheel problems. There is always an exception to the rule; in this case it was the introduction of King Class engines, which initially were dealt with on the factory road off the secondary turntable. In about 1946 it was then found that by lifting the leading bogie, access to the 35-ton end of the shop could be obtained via the traversing table.

The 'works' of the little broad-gauge engine 'Tiny' operated not only the machine shop machinery but also the fans for the blacksmith forges, the 25-ton capacity shaft-drive cranes in the erecting shop and a rope hoist for the handling wheel sets over the lathe. Heating and steam power came from two stationary boilers located between the smith shop and the machine shop. On the subject of heating, the erecting shop main doors faced almost due north and the blizzard-like blasts of air that blew in during the winter, when a locomotive came into the shop on the table, had to be experienced to be believed.

The posed repair picture depicting 4566 (p. xxx) shows the last 'heavy' repair undertaken. Repairs of a lighter nature continued for a short period. It is more than likely that the loco also received the usual 45XX Class treatment of a frame weld over the leading horns, as with the photograph of 5563. This weakness in the frames of the 45XX grouping formed a large proportion of the workload for the Newton Shops in the last years of steam.

Nationalisation other locos came and went after the required attention. The Southern Railway Merchant Navy Class graced the weighbridge on occasions as well as the standard classes allocated to the area. It was to be a short-lived steam scene after the haste to design standard locomotives. The diesel was creeping in everywhere and by 1967 the Newton Abbot steam scene had gone and the whole works had become unrecognisable internally. The traversing table was ripped out again (shades of 1893 after the broad gauge) and a new table installed across the end of the erecting shop, increasing the potential for cold blasts of air from more access doors. New diesel servicing buildings appeared and all shop functions altered. Even the steam-trained staff could only look back on the steam years as experience gained as their work changed dramatically.

This situation was occurring in all areas of the Great Western and is here taken to a conclusion as an example of events. Certain trades would of course be no longer required, or at best only a very limited requirement. Blacksmiths and boilermakers left or were retrained in other capacities, but the very existence of the works and staff hung under a dark cloud of uncertainty again.

With the departure of the last steam locomotive from the works, the complex had really entered its last phase. Diesel maintenance continued but during the next decade rumours were rife and speculation on closure was a main topic. During 1977 the Newton prospective Parliamentary candidate, in answer to queries, received a letter from the Chief Personnel Officer of British Rail seemingly confirming that 'nothing untoward is taking place at Newton Abbot' but mentioning the possibilities of some minor expansion of the Plymouth Laira Depot – assurances taken with the proverbial pinch of salt.

In January 1981 the rumours became fact with the news that the locomotive servicing and coach cleaning depot would close later in the year. The train crew depot was to close on 1 June, followed by the servicing and cleaning on 5 October. The £5m cost of the new depot at Laira had risen to £8m in four years and some justification for the expense was claimed by transferring the Newton Abbot work to the new site. Generally affected were forty-five footplate staff, thirty workshop staff, thirty carriage cleaners, eleven shunters and some clerical staff. As reported by the local newspaper, some staff would be transferred with the work.

The opening ceremony of the new Plymouth Laira Depot was really the closing down ceremony of the Newton Abbot Works. The whole site, as in other locations, became a vast speculative development area – its GWR associations now a note in the history books along with career details of one of its bright young men, G.J. Churchward.

As this is being written the works still exists, but neglect and vandalism are taking their toll. There is currently some new government thinking on the development and expansion of traffic by rail! The works may yet come back into its own as one of the few still remaining virtually intact.

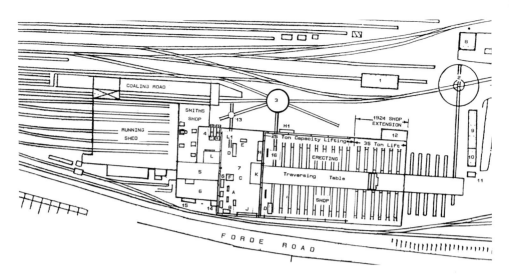

Newton Abbot workshops during the steam years.

Key

1   Weighbridge
2   Main turntable
3   Secondary turntable
4   Boiler room
5   Coppersmiths
6   Stores
7   Machine Shop

    A   Lathes
    B   Drills
    C   Milling machines
    D   Wheel lathe
    E   Shears
    F   Axle box boring machine
    G   Machine saw
    H   Superheater repair bench
    H1 Small component 'bosh'
    J   Motion repair gang
    K   Shop office (upstairs – foremen; downstairs – clerks & time office)
    L   Position prior to 1924 of the old broad gauge loco engine driving shafting for overhead crane and shop machinery
    L1 Shafting and overhead rope drive crane. Shafting also in old erecting shop (for cranes)

8   works' main pumphouse
9   messroom
10 MIS room
11 Time office until 1945, then boiler inspector's office
12 toilets
13 wheel turntable
14 ATC electricians' hut
15 bicycle shed
16 'King' class entry road

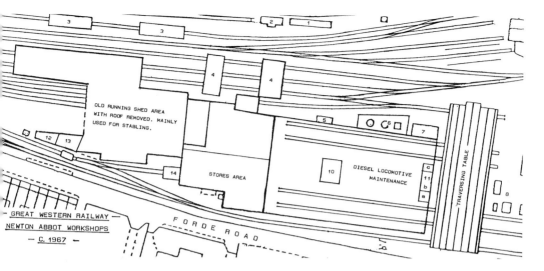

Newton Abbot workshops c. 1967 (diesel traction). The changing face of a workshop; all sign of the steam years is now completely gone.

Key

1 Carriage cleaners
2 DMU foreman's office
3 DMU servicing sheds
4 Fuelling sheds
5 First-aid room
6 Fuel storage tanks
7 Toilets
8 Coolant treatment sheds & tanks
9 Electrical substation
10 Oil & coolant sampling room
11 Office

    A Senior foreman
    B Supervisors (shift)
    C Documentation

12 AME office
13 Amenity block
14 Boiler house

No. 5563 in the shops for the usual 45XX Class treatment: a good weld-up of the frame over the leading horns, an inherent weak point in the class. This photograph of February 1960 illustrates a substantial portion of the workload at this end of the steam period.

A mix of repairs wait on the roads off the traverser outside the main doors. No. 5950 *Wardley Hall* has repair details chalked on the cylinder cladding.

A standard 2-6-0, No. 77006 running in from Swindon, stands outside the new amenity block in 1956. In less than ten years steam had officially gone.

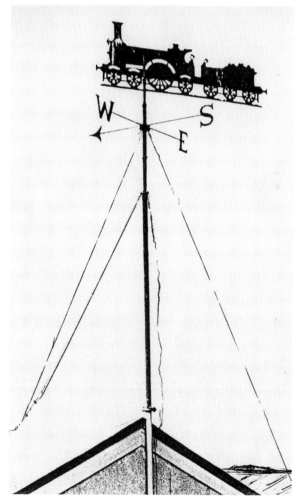

Newton Abbot factory weathervane.

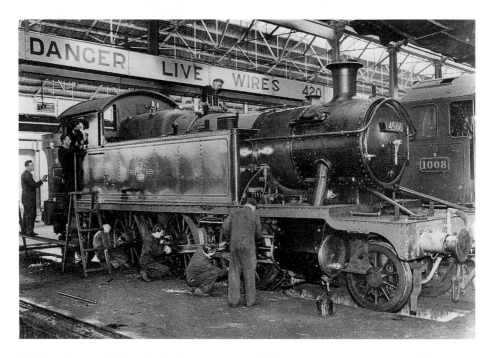

Work at Newton Abbot: the last heavy repair, 4566, gets last-minute attention. The new shop looks like Swindon's A(E) shop.

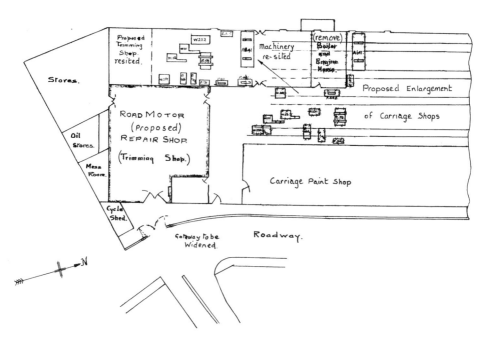

Newton Abbot – Proposed Addition (8 November 1928). Although not a locomotive workshop, this drawing indicated the increasing influence of road motor transport on the railway system. (This development was in the wagon & carriage section of the works, not shown on the other Newton Abbot Workshop plans.)

The abandoned works in 1991 with vandalism taking its toll, with a view down the old erecting shop toward the machine shop. The central bay was the traversing table road in steam days. Note the cranes still in situ, and the clock still in place but with its hands ripped off!

Outside the steam erecting shop. The centre glazed section is the old entry for the traversing table (showing conversions for the diesel era).

The erecting shop showing the 1924 brick extension (covering open-air tracks) added to the original stone-block building (with new end doors for diesel entry).

Abandoned works in 1991. Relics of the steam years – the end of the machine shop adjacent Forde Road. The ATC Electricians' hut rotting away. Note that through the window, the yellow-painted girder that carried the machine shop countershafts for driving the machinery.

Empty erecting shop converted for diesel use. Note the wall notice with red letters centre top; this was the separation point of the new and old shops. The notice reads '35 ton this side' on the left, and '25 ton this side' on the right. Note also the 'step' in the crane track separating the old shop from the new extension. The same crane covered the complete bay. (Crane 50-ton capacity restricted to weights shown.)

'Tiny', the sole broad-gauge survivor, during its working days at Newton Abbot works. It is still preserved after a further period as the power source driving machinery at the works.

Above and below: Mixed-gauge buffer stops and track. The former rotting away and the track unused and overgrown (photograph at Lelant, Cornwall *c.* 1908).

'Tiny' on station platform display.

7

Carn Brea, Cornwall – West Cornwall Railway

By a rather ironic twist of fate there were two Railway Bills before the House during 1834. One was to be ignominiously thrown out and the other was to go through without problems. The one rejected was for the GWR, and the success story goes to the Hayle Railway Company, a group with a £64,000 capital with powers to borrow a further £16,000. The intended line was to run from Hayle Foundry to the Transeavan Mine with branches to other mines and towns in the immediate area, to include Redruth and Portreath.

The line was for minerals from the mines served, but it was a railway with locomotives and not horses and it could carry passengers, the latter a very minor consideration on its inception. Maintenance was required for the mineral trucks and of course the locomotives, but until 1843 any passengers, and there were a considerable number, were presumably carried in the mineral trucks, as there were no passenger carriages! The accounting procedures were, to say the least, scrappy, and whilst the railway itself had changed hands by the time accounts were available, over 61,000 passengers are recorded in 1848 on a track less than 10 miles in length between Hayle and Redruth with branches and intermediate stops! If the figures are accurate, this seems an incredible mobility of population in such a small area.

A move by the newly formed West Cornwall Railway in 1846 to extend the Hayle coverage from both ends to cover Truro and Penzance and to be itself leased to the Hayle Company did not meet with approval. The positions were reversed and the West Cornwall absorbed the Hayle Railway instead. To save cash the line was to be narrow gauge with broad-gauge potential when finances permitted. Deviations in route were also implemented to cut out the assisted incline problems of the Hayle section and included the introduction of one of the first safety sidings with a 'sand drag' section installed in the mid 1850s.

The broad-gauge rail was a long time coming and still no money was available. The only course was amalgamation or takeover, and an association with the GWR, the Bristol & Exeter and the South Devon Railway was formed in 1866; the broad-gauge trains being able to run to Penzance by the end of the year. The last broad-gauge track laid as new was a short stretch on this line into St Ives.

The alteration to parts of the original Hayle route had removed several canal-type obstacles from a potential free traffic flow. To cope with terrain problems several 'inclined planes' had been installed. These powered, rope-assisted inclines added considerably to costs not only in installation and maintenance but also in the provision and running of stationary engines as a power boost. One particularly steep section excluded locomotives altogether at Hayle Wharf, which in the early days was worked by horses. The takeover by the West Cornwall Railway was one of the triumphs of broad gauge. It now meant that a broad-gauge train could journey from Paddington to Penzance without the break of gauge at Truro. The whole was still complicated by 4ft 8½in trains, and between Truro and Penzance a mixed-gauge freight service operated using a mix of broad- and narrow-gauge trucks with a special 'joint' truck with sliding buffers and coupling. This allowed a snail's pace double shuffle of trucks when points were encountered!

On takeover the five locomotives of the Hayle Railway were also the first on the West Cornwall tracks. These were followed by Stephenson 2-4-0 tender designs and four six-coupled locos purchased from the London & North Western Railway.

With amalgamation the Hayle Railway's main workshops at Carn Brea became the new company's repair and manufacturing centre. The latter activity was of a very limited nature. Whilst repair facilities existed with the usual lathes and drilling machines within the inevitable smithy, activities were restricted to 'building' as opposed to actually 'making' locomotives. In the early 1850s, and with a life of about twelve years, three locomotives were built to possibly 2-4-0 format with 5ft drivers and 16 × 24in cylinders. Whilst some manufacturing of small parts could have been done at Carn Brea, the main items were supplied by the Bristol locomotive firm of Stothert & Slaughter. Having got the three locomotives out of the shop by 1855 the routine settled into a maintenance function for about ten years until in 1865, a burst of manufacturing activity produced a six-coupled goods loco with outside frames, its component parts also supplied from outside, probably again by Stothert & Slaughter.

The West Cornwall Railway was absorbed by the Great Western in 1876 having been part of the controlling association for ten years. Its last locomotive building effort, the 0-6-0, was rebuilt by the GW (at Newton Shops) into a broad-gauge saddle tank.

There appears to have been some rebuilding in 1879 or thereabouts, and the function changed somewhat on takeover. The blacksmith facilities, which must have existed in the original layout, were presumably considered inadequate (or antiquated?) in the 1890s. They were replaced in 1896 by a designated 14 × 22ft smithy, along with improved sand drying, water and coaling facilities.

The shops remained in use for locomotive repair and maintenance until the complete function was transferred to Truro in 1902, when the role was relegated to that of wagon repairs. The shops closed in 1917, having had a reducing maintenance role from the date of transfer at the beginning of the century.

The original workshops and offices of the Hayle Railway were much larger in extent that the late photographs indicate. In 1880, it is recorded as a carriage works. At this time it boasted loco or carriage workshops, a large general office, a workshop/stores building and a number of short storage rail tracks from both sides of a long-travel traversing table, covering both of the rail fed workshops. At the time of writing the only available information indicated a mixed-gauge line from the main to a locomotive shed, presumably the old broad-gauge shed. On the opposite side of the main line stands a narrow-gauge shed. The original complete works was surrounded by a number of traditional Cornish mine engine houses with their bobbing beams working the whims, pump and ore stamps, the works named from the adjacent hill Carn Brea.

Whilst most passenger trains – five on weekdays and two on Sundays – were broad gauge, there was a daily Truro/Penzance return, which was narrow gauge up until 1871. Goods traffic was nearly all narrow gauge, with one through broad-gauge train for perishables, and other perishables transhipped at Truro to narrow gauge. Mineral trains were narrow gauge on main or branches, and the Carn Brea Yard and Workshops stabled and maintained the stock.

Also made in the shops would have been the unusual match wagons, which by special buffers and sliding couplings allowed a train of mixed stock, broad and narrow, to operate carefully but successfully on the mixed-gauge track.

As the Hayle Railway became part of the West Cornwall Railway so in 1876 the West Cornwall became part of the Great Western and the role of Carn Brea Workshops changed. Major locomotive repairs, such as the previously mentioned rebuilding or completion of the two locos under construction at Carn Brea, transferred to Newton Abbot on takeover. Its diminishing workload included use of part of the works as carriage shops and was a feature of the change of duties, locomotive servicing continuing for a period after takeover.

From the 1880 period of use for carriage repairs, major demolitions or disposals must have occurred. By 1908 much of the original works had gone. The large stores/workshop/office block, and the traverser-fed second workshop (C on the plan, p.129), had disappeared along with the traverser itself. The broad and narrow gauge running sheds had also been demolished, the loco shed such as it was now a part of the old workshop. By closure in 1917 only two very small buildings remained. One building was a two-track loco shed and the other a single-track wagon repair shop.

By the 1960s all the mines in the area had long since closed and the railway works site had become an industrial estate.

Above: The Carn Brea Works and sheds on the West Cornwall Railway. *Below*: All that remained of the Carn Brea Works at the time of closure in 1917.

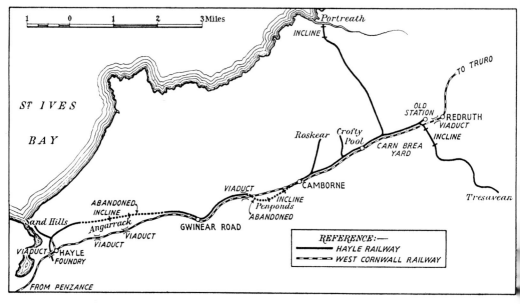

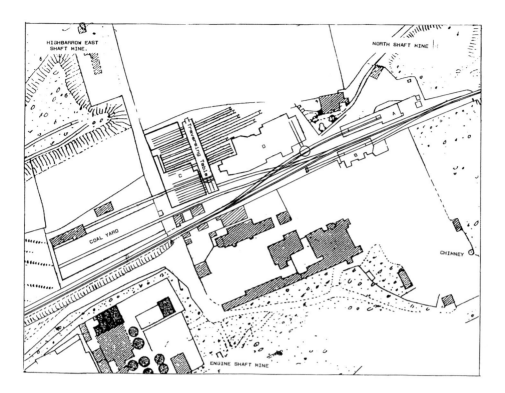

The GWR workshops at Carn Brea c. 1880, originally the shops of the Hayle Railway (1834), absorbed by the West Cornwall Railway (1846) and by the Great Western Railway (1876). By 1880 it was in use as a carriage works, which closed in 1917.

Key

A Old broad-guage (now mixed-gauge) loco shed
B Standard-gauge shed
C Carriage shops
D Stores, fitting and machine shops (?)

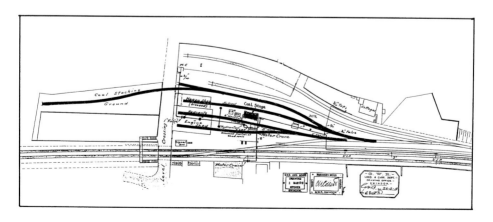

GWR Carn Brea Yard, 1918.

8

Worcester Workshops

A Great Western constituent company in a rather roundabout fashion was the Oxford, Worcester & Wolverhampton Railway. The workshops located at Worcester were to take some time to become organised, a feature of many of the early railway companies. The efforts of starting the railway and reaching a stage when it started to give returns on capital meant that such things as workshop facilities, as indeed actual maintenance itself, were among those expenses pushed into the background. Whether or not this was in the hope it would go away, it was also associated with distinct shortages of money.

Started in 1845, the Oxford, Worcester & Wolverhampton Railway opened its shops in 1854, but obtaining the necessary equipment was a slower process. It was the beginning of the 1860s before the first loco rolled out through the doors. Early construction efforts were not really pressed, the first out being a conglomerate use of second-hand materials from the first, and now withdrawn, locomotives had been built by Hawthorns. Having produced or extensively rebuilt their first batch of three 0-6-0s, the railway's command structure changed on incorporation with the Worcester & Hereford and the Newport, Abergavenny & Hereford, the triple amalgamation producing the West Midland Railway.

Two years later in 1862, the last locomotives rolled out: this time four 0-6-0s, much like the three previously rehashed. The West Midland Railway lasted independently for about another year when it came within the grasp of the GW and the workload was transferred to the Stafford Road Works as the West Midland was absorbed. However, a great amount moved back again for repairs and maintenance only, as the Stafford Road establishment had encompassed the actual building function for any future new stock, but could not cope with all of the other requirements.

Actual locomotive building at Worcester is really a misnomer; as with most 'rebuilds' the incorporation of many existing components turned the whole programme into almost one of very heavy general repairs. Whilst much can be done with a good smiths' shop associated with a general run of the machine tools of the day, the actual manufacture of the bigger components was beyond the capabilities of a number of workshops of the smaller railway companies. Heavy forging and casting facilities were costly to install and maintain, and without a definite construction programme such expense was not justified.

With the absorption of the West Midland Railway into the GW, a number of the associated management, clerical and craft staff were not required, as work was transferred to other areas. The superintendent of what had been the Oxford, Worcester & Wolverhampton carriage and wagon department, in association with an administration officer and an entrepreneur, formed an engineering business at the Shrub Hill Vulcan Ironworks. This combination proved quite successful as the founders, with good technical and administrative skills went from strength to strength.

A much more grandiose works – the Worcester Engine Works – was also a product of surplus staff following the merger of the West Midland Railway and the GWR. Further endorsed by the massive fire that destroyed the carriage works, the transfer of even more work had caused the redundancy of many more craft and executive personnel. The efforts to continue locomotive and rolling-stock building with a newly formed company, after a promising year from the start of 1864, saw the order book slowly disintegrate, and the company went out of business in 1871. Among the locomotives supplied had been a small batch of convertibles, narrow to broad gauge and back again, for the Bristol & Exeter Railway. The efforts with the new company to continue employment in familiar products had sadly failed. During this recession period, the West Central Wagon Company also went into liquidation – another severe blow to local employment. Now only the buildings remained for future development, outside the scope of this book.

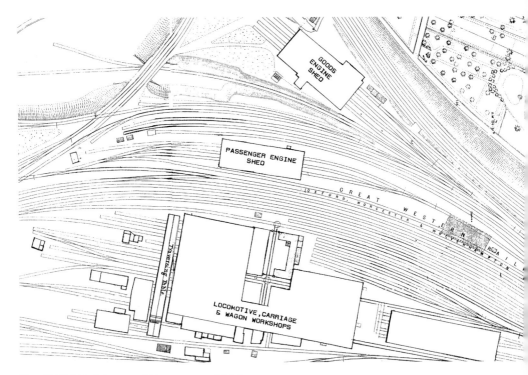

The GWR Workshops at Worcester, *c.* 1884.

Opposite: The GWR Workshops at Worcester, *c.* 1926 (showing very little change from the layout o
1884).

Key

1 Station master's house
2 Running shed foreman's office
3 Goods engine shed
4 fitters' shop
5 Toilets
6 Chargeman, fitter & boilermaker
7 brick store (boiler arch)
8 hand 10-ton hoist & covered benches
9 Divisional, loco and carriage & wagon works' superintendent's office. Also sheet works & store
manager's office
10 Hand cart repair shop
11 Civil engineer's workshop
12 Wagon repairer's hut
13 Time office & staff messroom
14 Carriage and wagon works examiner's cabin
15 cycle shed

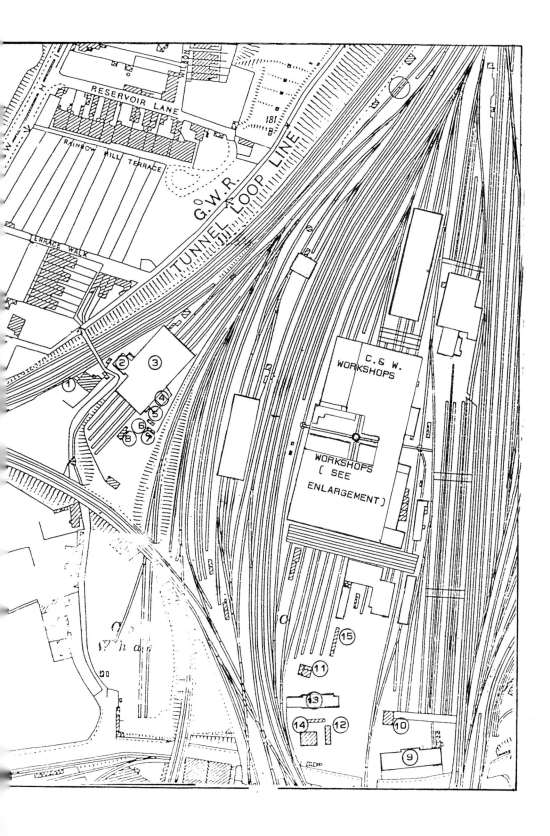

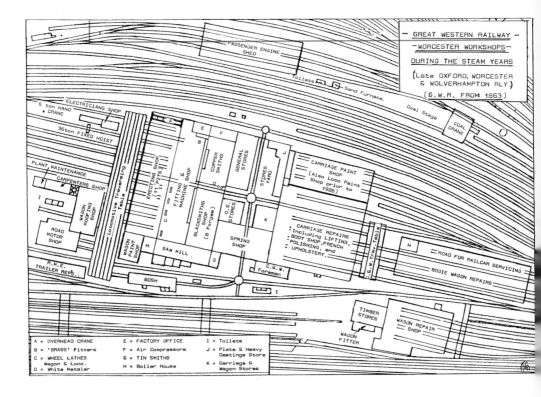

The GWR's Worcester Workshops during the steam years (Late Oxford, Worcester &
Wolverhampton Railway – GWR from 1863).

Key

A Overhead crane
B Brass fitters
C Wheel lathes – wagon & loco
D White metaler
E Factory office
F Air compressors
G Tin smiths
H Boiler house
I Toilets
J Plate and heavy castings store
K Carriage and wagon stores

Worcester repair shops and loco yard – 1945.

lo. 6819 *Highnam Grange* (with no name plate!) under the hoist at Worcester Works.

9

Some Other Miscellaneous Maintenance Facilities

The previous pages recounted in brief detail the basic history of those works that actually built steam locomotives, albeit in their independent company existence before takeover by the Great Western. At other strategic sites, locomotive repair facilities were developed or installed to ease the burden on the main works facilities, increasing in number as the Great Western itself expanded. Around the turn of the century this growth triggered a move for a standardised format of repair shop. G.J. Churchward introduced such designs to facilitate both ease of construction of the shops themselves, and to enable a selected range of repairs to locomotives to be carried out in the areas where they actually worked. All of these arrangements were thus designed to not only ease the burden on the main works but reduce movement and paperwork.

Whilst the locations of the workshops varied as new buildings were erected or existing buildings were updated, the nature of the repairs to the locomotives did not really alter within the context of workshop design from place to place. In this way any photographs of work undertaken in such shops show the same operations, reflecting the essential but basic repairs such shops were designed to do. There are numerous photographs of locomotives under the various types of hoist, with bogies removed or wheels being taken out. There are the inevitable long wooden boxes containing piston valves recorded somewhere on the photographs, along with the inevitable shot of piston valves removed and being dealt with on the benches. Attention to the very wide rings of the piston valves is also much in evidence.

The locomotives themselves were straight off the road and into the lifting shops, so cleaning before attention was a hand-scraper-and-oily-cotton-waste job; there were no big tanks of caustic soda and steam in which to immerse the complete bogie assembly to remove the grime, as at a main works. Machining facilities were also limited. In the smaller lifting shops a lathe – possibly an old one removed from a main works – a large pillar and/or a radial drill, a double-headed grind stone and maybe a shaper – again second-hand from a main works – usually completed the machining capabilities. The indispensable blacksmith was available, ranging from a single hearth in a small lifting shop to several hearths in one of the larger arrangements, set out in a separate shop.

Secondary but main divisional works such as Old Oak, Ebbw and Tyseley had good workshop equipment with a range of machine tools and good, although single hoist, overhead crane facilities were also found in some of the smaller shops. Even the later and much larger divisional shops were not involved in 'building' locomotives. Lifting shops themselves were all built adjacent to or as a separate section of the locomotive running shed itself. Thus the attention of the fitting and maintenance staff was always at hand, the larger shops capable of a heavier degree of locomotive maintenance.

The following pages and illustrations reflect some of the various designs of lifting shops that dealt with steam repairs and some of the activities and personnel who undertook such work.

Old Oak Common

Although not 'making' locomotives in the true sense of the word, we should mention the layout of the shops and sheds at Old Oak Common, constructed during the three or four years up to 1906 and replacing the older layout at Westbourne Park. It was at the latter that Daniel Gooch had a temporary office before moving to Paddington – the layout replacing the earlier facility with its circular shed at Bishops Road, Paddington. It was here that Brunel and Gooch laboured to get the first locos roadworthy, realigning and rebuilding blast pipes and nozzles to improve steaming on the earlier and not too successful motive power.

The Westbourne Park layout housed and succoured famous GW names, among them *North Star* and later *Lord of the Isles* both to be ignominiously destroyed fifty years later. The 'Park' had eventually both narrow (4ft 8½in) and broad (7ft 0¼in) sheds. The latter shed had a unique turntable; steam operated from an adjacent engine and boiler house and driven by a chain around its periphery. A sprocket wheel in the engine house meshed with the chains and the usual pushing and shoving by the train crew was not required.

The 1906 successor of the two earlier depots, that at Old Oak, included a repair and lifting shop 195ft × 101ft and twelve pits 52ft long. A strip 45ft down one complete length housed the fitting and machine bay and an overhead single-lift crane served the locomotive pits. Outside ran an 80-ton-capacity traversing table, all machinery and lifting/traversing items electrically powered. Whilst the main works at Swindon struggled along with gas lighting, the new Old Oak Shop was equipped with electric light – both DC and AC – used for open-type double-carbon arc lamps controlled in groups.

Power, incidentally, would be supplied from the 1902 Great Western generating station at Park Royal, built originally for the electrical working of the line between Bishops Road and Hammersmith. The first use of electricity for lighting railway property was at Paddington and adjacent yards and offices, from plant established as early as 1886. Whilst this was not easy to manage, nor very economical, it was nevertheless successful and a real pioneer installation.

Other workshops at Old Oak included a 74ft × 47ft smiths' shop, 61ft × 23ft carpenters' shop and a 61ft × 23ft coppersmiths' shop. Large stores and office accommodation were provided for this most comprehensive and up-to-date addition to the London end of the GW complex. This 'standard' design of large repair shop was followed at Ebbw and Tyseley.

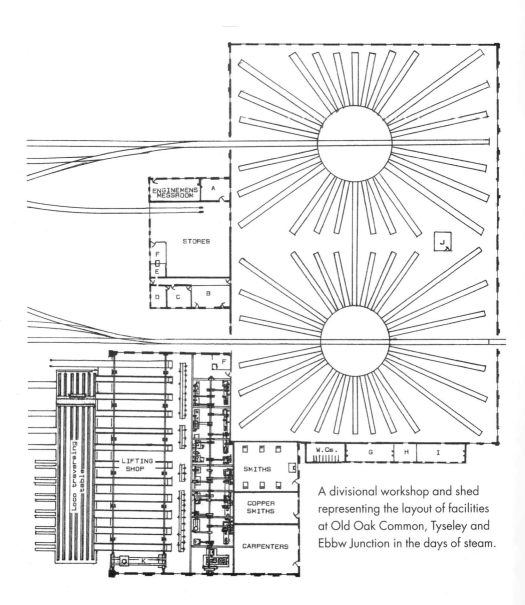

A divisional workshop and shed representing the layout of facilities at Old Oak Common, Tyseley and Ebbw Junction in the days of steam.

French loco *Alliance* under the hoist at Old Oak Common, *c.* 1906.

Note the condition of the uncleaned bogie under repair.

Work in progress on piston valves.

View across the shop.

King William II No. 6007: preparing to lift engine by overhead travelling crane. Note the old-type wheel lathe in the background with its own individual shaft and belt drive.

Old Oak Common: A general view.

The bogie is rolled out.

Fitting new rings to a piston valve.

Tyseley

Following alterations at Birmingham around 1908 the engine shed at Bordesley was vacated and a new complex built at Tyseley. The new shed was accompanied by a new large lifting shop following the design of that at Old Oak Common: 197ft × 112ft with twelve pits each 52ft long. The pits were served by an overhead crane of 35 tons' capacity and 23ft above the shop floor. Among the general facilities were a smiths' shop with six single hearths, a double hearth and a spring furnace. The usual offices and mess rooms were provided along with a carpenters' shop and coppersmiths' shop.

Power for machinery, crane and outside traverser was delivered rather cleverly from one gas engine! This double-ended source drove shafting direct by a clutch from one end, whilst the other end powered a DC generator of 75kw (100bhp). Some machines with motors of 8–40hp were also powered from this generator if they were outside the positioning of the main mechanical drive shafting.

Machinery in workshops, up to say the last quarter century of steam, was nearly always adjacent to a wall or row of roof columns. This gave support to the long lengths of shafting and countershafting and miles of flapping flat belt that drove the machinery of the shops. At Tyseley, as an example, the machinery was in two parallel rows under a framework of steel section channel and angle utilising the usual wall for one of the rows.

One long shaft above the centre line of the frame drove the countershaft arrangements of the double row of machinery (see p.39.)

As with many depots, Tyseley closed to steam traffic early in 1967; the running shed shut in 1970 and all locomotives and crews moved to Saltley. On final shutdown Tyseley became a traction maintenance depot (TMD). The old carriage shed survived until early 1973 and by 1977 mainline coaches were dealt with elsewhere. Tyseley itself became one of the largest diesel multiple unit depots. The steam shops are now the Birmingham Railway Museum, sandwiched between the diesel multiple unit depot and the TMD, both the latter being outside the scope of this book but within sight and sound of steam.

General view of the buildings at Tyseley.

General view of the engine repair bay looking very neat and tidy!

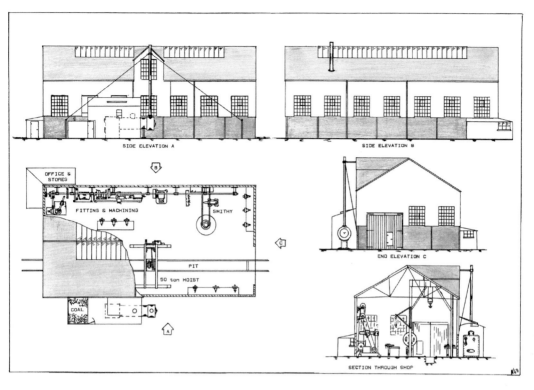

A representative standard lifting shop for steam locomotives.

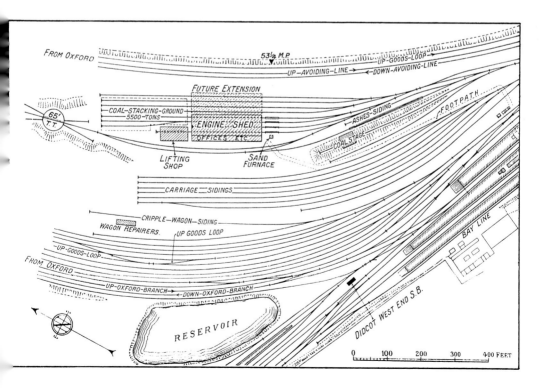

Site plan of Didcot shed and lifting shop in the 1930s (see also above picture).

The Didcot lifting shop still operating for the Great Western Society.

Didcot lifting shop with the 'resurrection of steam', a typical application thirty years after its official demise.

Wheel removal under the hoist.

Operating the 'new' lathe installed behind the original (still operative).

Kingfisher (No. 3448) under the hoist in the original and very new Didcot lifting shop.

Didcot lifting shop: detail of the 10/50-ton hoist.

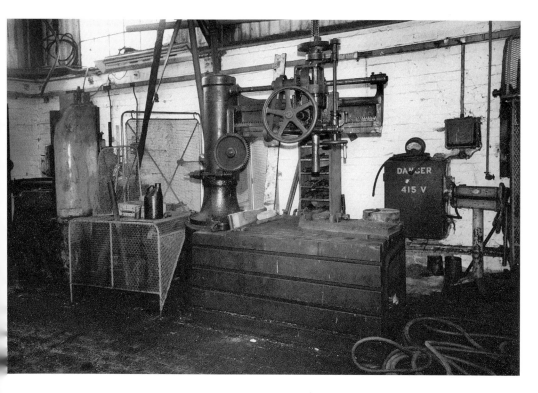

Recycled machine tools in use once again for steam repairs (Didcot GWS Workshops): a drilling machine (*c.* 1870 design) and a shaper.

The Boston Lodge shops of the Ffestiniog Railway. This railway has a long history, starting life as a horse plateway following the establishment of a packhorse route. Further improvements (1808–11) included the building of a sea wall (known as the 'cob') and establishing a new harbour at Porthmadog. For a quarter-century the horses plodded along the plateway. The building in 1832 of a new railway of 1ft 11½in gauge opened up a new 14-mile route, with further updating in 1859 with the introduction of two small 0-4-0 steam locomotives. Brunel and Stephenson both insisted that steam could not work on such a small gauge, but both were proved wrong. In 1870 the introduction of the double-ended 'Fairlie' design of locomotive carried steam forward. Closing for passenger traffic in 1939, the route was abandoned in 1946. Opened again by enthusiasts in the mid 1950s, it is now a profitable tourist success story. Surrounded as it was by GWR lines, it was listed as a 'foreign' line in 1926.

The Danygraig shops of the late Rhonda & Swansea Bay Railway (c. 1925). Note the rope-drive overhead crane and the lack of room between the centre track and the pit roads on either side.

The Barry Workshops of the Barry Railway: the wheel and machine shop in the 1920s.

Boiler repairs at Barry Workshops (1954).

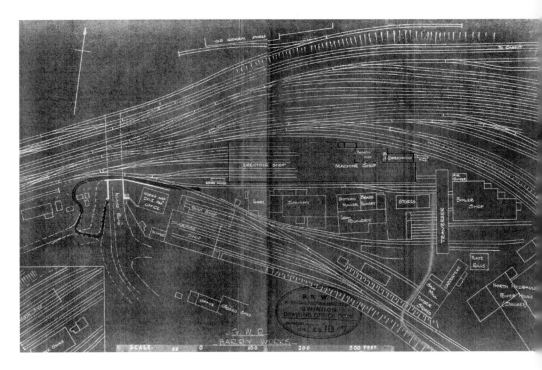

Great Western Railway, Barry Workshops (late Barry Dock & Railway Co. – GWR from 1922).

Repairs in the open. Attention to a safety valve for *Otterington Hall* (No. 6983) in 1963.

A Churchward lifting shop under construction in 1915 at Westbury, Wiltshire (closed 1965).

smiths' shop at Cardiff Cathays carrying out mainly carriage and wagon work – Taff Vale Railway 1920s).

An example of one of the smaller workshops, this photograph shows the inside of the shop at Exeter in around 1935. Note the engine for driving the line shaft for the machinery (right foreground) and a typical bench and leg vise arrangement for the fitters, with a single-lift hydraulic overhead crane over the rail tracks. The long box and those back left are for the transportation of piston valves. A railway operating division ('ROD') loco receives attention, a survivor of the First World War.

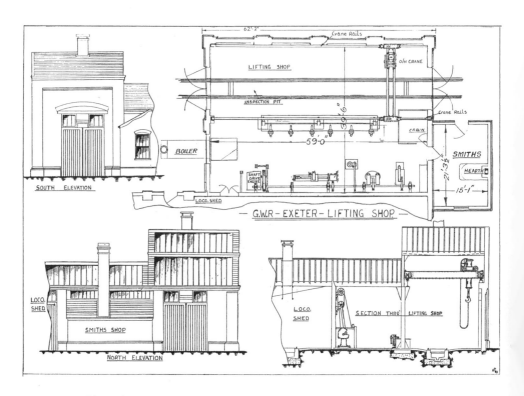

GWR Exeter lifting shop.

Loco in the open for repairs to the trailing drivers, *c.* 1950. A hot box? Also not good for the front bogie suspension! A hoist positioned outside the shed was pleasant in the summer but not so good on a Monday morning in an icy winter.

Tyseley in 2012: this locomotive, *Earl of Mountedgecombe*, has been returned to superb condition and is now main line steaming. A great credit to Bob

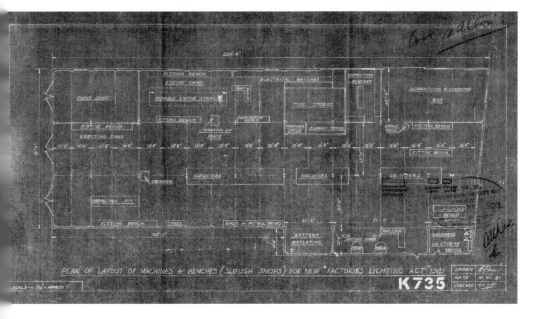

The GWR road motor transport workshops at Slough (1941).

The increasing influence of road transport on the GWR: the GWR road transport workshops at Slough during the 1920s.

Fitting and machining section at Slough.

PART 4

1

Maintenance Facilities

The following selection of layout plans and operating details will give a broad outline of the day-to-day working of the varied design of lifting shops in a selected area.

Carmarthen Depot (Neath Division)

Locomotives, on entering the yard, proceed direct to coaling road, where ashes are unloaded to the ash flat from whence they are manually loaded into wagons standing on adjacent siding. Coaling is effected from an elevated coaling platform 11ft 6in above coaling road rail. This distance can be increased to 14ft 0in by means of an electric lift at the tipping point. Half-ton capacity coal tubs are used on the platform.

The average weekly make of ash is seven wagons, and the coal consumption is 500 tons per week.

For turning, locomotives proceed to a 65ft manually operated turntable, and return to a six-road 'dead end' shop.

Steam for hot water boiler washing purposes etc. is drawn from two stationary boilers.

The repair shop contains two pit roads and is equipped with a 30-ton overhead crane, operated by means of electrically driven shafting and belt. Smithing and machining facilities are also provided.

The water supply for locomotives is obtained from a 74,250-gallon storage tank situated over the coal stage and feed columns adjacent to the shed and table. The water for boiler washing is also drawn from this supply.

The tank is supplied by gravitation from a reservoir fed by a stream. Water delivered by pump from the River Towy forms a supplementary supply. Drinking water is obtained from the local authority.

Total number of engines allocated – 46:		**Staff:**	
4-6-0	13	Supervisors	3
2-8-0	5	Clerical	4
2-6-0	2	Drivers	77
0-6-0	6	Firemen	76
2-6-2T	5	Cleaners	11
0-6-0T	11	Shed Grades	33
0-4-2T	2	Fitters & Mates	27
		Boilersmiths & Mates	54

Summary of work performed:

Passenger and freight services – local or semi-local in character – Carmarthen/Neyland, Carmarthen/Swansea, etc. Partially fitted vacuum freight services to Bristol and Paddington.

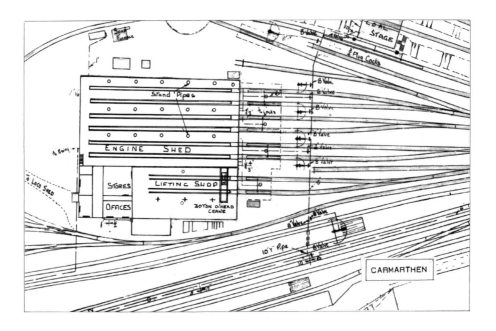

Landore Depot (Neath Division)

Locomotives normally enter the yard from the Landore station end of the yard and proceed to two roads leading to a double-sided, elevated platform-type coal stage. Ashes are dropped on the respective ash flats from whence they are loaded into wagons standing on adjacent roads. Coaling tubs of ½-ton capacity are used on the coaling platforms, the height of which above the coaling roads rail level is 13ft on the side nearest the sheds and 14ft on the other.

The week's make of ash is twelve wagons, and 900 tons of coal are loaded to locos weekly.

For turning locos a 65ft manually operated turntable is located behind the end of an elevated coal wagon road, from which point locos return to shed. The shed farthest from the table, being the older of the two, containing four 'dead end' pit roads and the shed nearest the table being of later construction also has four 'dead end' pit roads.

Hot water boiler-washing facilities are provided, steam being obtained from a boiler house containing two boilers, situated at the front end of the repair shop.

The repair shop, which has one pit road, is equipped with a 50-ton electrically driven hoist, together with machining and smithing arrangements.

The loco water supply is pumped from the Swansea canal and is supplemented by a gravitation supply from a reservoir. The storage tank of 45,000 gallons capacity is sited over the coal stage and supplies columns and a boiler washing hydrant etc.

Drinking water is obtained by means of a metered supply from the corporation mains.

A loco oil fuel plant (on a care and maintenance basis at present) exists at this depot, consisting of two storage tanks and a pump-house etc., steam being obtained from the loco shed boiler-washing steam main.

Total number of engines allocated – 62:		**Staff:**	
4-6-0	26	Supervisors	4
2-8-2T	5	Clerical	7
2-6-2T	3	Drivers	126
0-6-2T	7	Firemen	127
0-6-0T	17	Cleaners	27
Diesel Cars	4	Shed Grades	47
		Fitters & Mates	28
		Boilersmiths & Mates	8

Summary of work performed:

Main-line express passenger services to Cardiff and to London. Also, local passengers. Freight services, mainly with heavy tank engines to Cardiff, Newport, Severn Tunnel Junction etc.

Severn Tunnel Junction (Newport Division)

Independent in and out roads give access to the yard, the incoming side of which has a double-sided coal stage. Locomotives ash drop, then proceed to the loco shed. There are two tipping points 63ft apart, giving a tipping height of 13ft above pit road level; the other side has one tipping point 10ft above rail level, which can be further increased to 14ft by means of an electric hoist. On the platform ½-ton-capacity coal tubs are used.

Coal consumption is 1,093 tons and twenty wagons of ashes are loaded weekly.

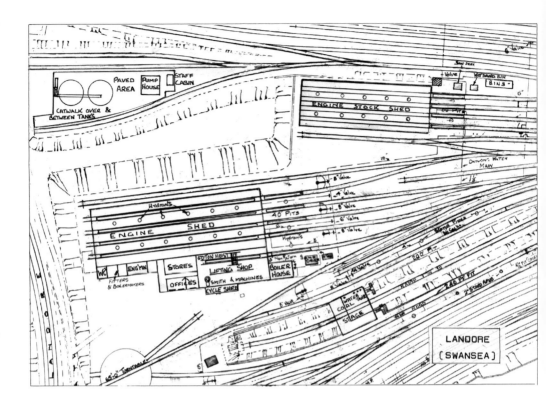

After coaling all locos can if necessary be turned on the 65ft-diameter turntable. Also locos coaling on the side facing the shed can bypass the table before they proceed to the rear of the loco shed.

The shed contains six pit roads, which are connected at both ends, thereby allowing for 'through' working.

Hot water boiler-washing is carried out with hard water heated with steam drawn from the boiler house, which contains two boilers and is situated at the rear of the shed.

The repair shop is a separate building, having one through road with a 35-ton electric hoist positioned over the pit. The shop is equipped for machining and smithing work.

The water supply for the yard and the district is obtained from the Severn Tunnel, the pumping station being at Sudbrook, some 3 miles distant. The water is chlorinated for drinking purposes and the loco water is softened in the softener at the west end of the loco yard. The storage tank over the coal stage is partitioned to form two tanks of 22,500 gallons each, one being for softened and the other for hard water.

Total number of engines allocated – 62:

4-6-0	2
2-8-0	24
2-6-0	2
0-6-0	2
2-8-2T	9
2-8-0T	10
2-6-2T	23
0-6-2T	11
0-6-0T	8

Staff:

Supervisors	6
Clerical	M 11 / F 1
Engine Recorders	3
Drivers	217
Firemen	191
Cleaners	11
Shed Grades	76
Fitters & Mates	42
Boilersmiths & Mates	11

Summary of work performed:

Main-line coal and freight services to all areas. Services to Swansea Division principally by tank engines. One passenger engine turn only. Severn Tunnel bank engines. Shunting engines for hump yards.

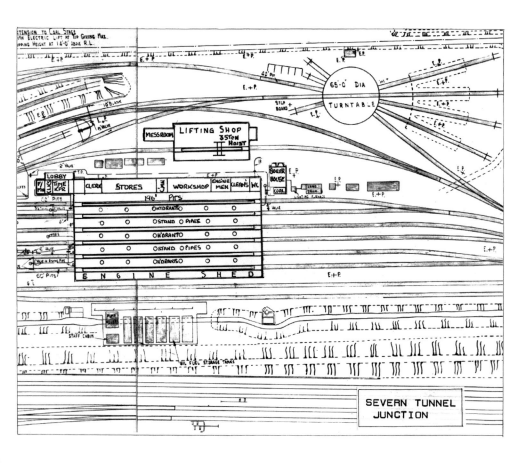

SEVERN TUNNEL JUNCTION

Pontypool Road Depot (Newport Division)

Access from the running lines is provided at four points, giving direct connections towards the station or alternatively for the siding nests. The locomotives approach the coaling stage on the ash pit road over which ashes are dropped. Coaling is effected from the elevated, single-sided platform-type stage, which is 11ft 6in high and along the side of which are three tipping points for the ½-ton capacity wheeled coal tubs. At the central tip an electric lift is provided, which increases the tipping height to14ft. Coal consumption is 970 tons and the make of ash is twenty wagons per week.

After coaling, locomotives proceed to a single-unit turntable shed.

The turntable – 55ft in diameter – serves twenty-four radiating roads, two of which are nominally access roads, while the third forms a connecting road leading to an eight-road straight-type shed, which is attached to the turntable shed. A boiler fixed in the turntable shed supplies steam for hot water boiler-washing etc.

Repairing facilities, located in the turntable shed, consist of a 30-ton hydraulic hoist together with machining and smithing arrangements.

The loco water supply is drawn by gravitation from the nearby Brecon & Merthyr Canal (owned by the Transport Commission), the loco yard storage tank having a capacity of 40,300 Gallons. Drinking water is obtained from the local water authority.

Total number of engines allocated – 89:

4-6-0	7
2-8-0	22
2-6-0	5
0-6-0	1
2-8-2T	6
2-8-0T	1
2-6-2T	8
0-6-2T	7
0-6-0T	31
0-4-2T	1
Diesel Cars	1

Staff:

Supervisors	8
Clerical	M 11 / F 2
Drivers	202
Firemen	189
Cleaners	22
Shed Grades	59
Fitters & Mates	38
Boilersmiths & Mates	7

Sub-depots:

Branches Fork – 2 engines, 0-6-0T type

Pontrillas – 1 engine, 0-4-2T type

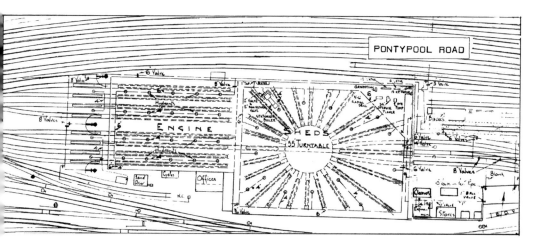

Summary of work performed:

Main-line freight services to Birmingham Division, Chester etc. Local passenger and freight working on the Vale of Neath section etc.

Ebbw Junction Depot (Newport Division)

Locomotives entering the yard proceed under the bridge to a spur and then reverse on to the coaling roads of a double-sided coal stage. The platforms of the coal stage, on which wheeled coal tubs are used, are 12ft above coaling road rail level. This tipping height is increased to 14f by means of an electric lift placed at the tip. After ash dropping and coaling, locomotives proceed to a twin-unit turntable shed. The two 65ft turntables are interconnected and each has twenty-eight radiating roads of varying lengths. Independent incoming and outgoing roads lead to the tables. In the main, passenger locos use one side of the coal stage and its attendant turntable while freight locos use the other side. 1,380 tons of coal are loaded to locos per each week, the make of ash being twenty wagons.

The repair shop has twelve pit roads (a traversing table serving eleven) and is equipped with a 35-ton overhead electric crane with extensive machining and smithing facilities. Two boilers, together with a boiler in the loco shed, supply the steam requirements at this depot, including steam for hot water boiler-washing. The water supply is drawn from the storage tank over the coal stage, which has a capacity of 146,000 gallons and is supplied from the Newport Corporation mains.

A loco oil-fuelling plant at this depot, consisting of six horizontal tanks and pump house, etc., is on a 'care and maintenance' basis.

Total number of engines allocated – 148:

4-6-0	12
2-8-0	24
2-6-0	1
0-6-0	4
2-8-2T	11
2-8-0T	32
2-6-2T	7
0-6-2T	10
0-6-0T	46
0-4-2T	1
Diesel Cars	2

Staff

Supervisors	8
Clerical	M 16 / F 2
Engine Recorders	3
Drivers	256
Firemen	243
Cleaners	43
Shed Grades	131
Fitters & Mates	61
Fitters & Mates Shop Staff	41
Boilersmiths & Mates	20
Boilersmiths & Mates Shop Staff	2

Summaro of Work Performed

Main-line coal and freight services. Coal services under control orders to and from western valleys, etc. Small number of local passenger services.

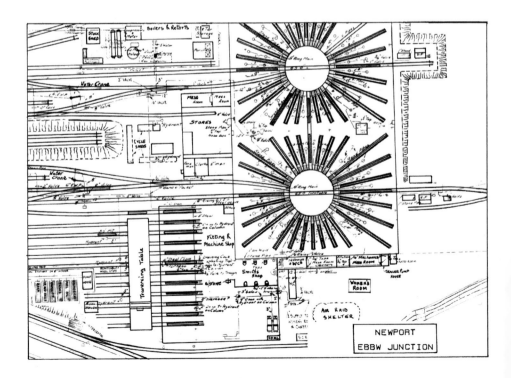

NEWPORT
EBBW JUNCTION

Cardiff (Canton) Depot (Newport Division)

Incoming locomotives normally enter the yard from the direction of Cardiff General Station and so proceed direct to the ash dropping and coaling road. Locomotives of trains terminating at the station usually draw the trains into the carriage shed and proceed via the road adjacent to the turntable, through the ash shelter on the road nearest the lifting shop and so to the ashing and coaling road. The coal stage, with three coal tipping points spaced along the single-sided platform, gives a tipping height of about 14ft above the coaling road level.

Quick-turnaround locomotives can be catered for. They can enter the yard and gain the outside turntable off an independent road from the running line, then return to the pit sited on the third road from the coal stage. A coaling station is available on this road by means of a covered gantry from the coal stage, 13ft 10in high, over which the coal tubs can be propelled.

The weekly coal consumption is 1,998 tons, and in this period twenty-five wagons of ashes are loaded.

After coaling, the larger types of locomotives (principally passenger) turn on the 65ft outside turntable and are the stabled in the straight shed, which contains six pit roads. The other locomotives proceed to the inside table (55ft in diameter), frpm which radiate twenty-nine roads.

Steam for hot water boiler washing is obtained from a stationary boiler in the turntable shed.

The repair shop, which is adjacent to the turntable shed , is provided with a 35-ton electric hoist, machining and smithing equipment.

The water supply is obtained from the Cardiff corporation and stored in a 45,000-gallon-capacity tank situated off the front end of the straight shed.

A loco oil-fuelling plant, consisting of two vertical storage tanks with pump and boiler house etc., is situated between the outside turntable and the sheds, and is on a 'care and maintenance' basis at present.

Total number of engines allocated – 110:		**Staff:**	
4-6-0	36	Supervisors	7
2-8-0	17	Clerical	M 14 / F 2
2-6-0	6	Engine Recorders	3
0-6-0	3	Drivers	307
2-8-2T	2	Firemen	279
2-8-0T	14	Cleaners	43
2-6-2T	1	Shed Grades	91
0-6-2T	12	Fitters & Mates	63
0-6-0T	19	Boilersmiths & Mates	15

Summary of work performed:

Main-line express passenger services to London, Bristol, Birmingham, Shrewsbury, Swansea etc. Also local passenger services. Main-line and local freight services, including partially fitted vacuum freights.

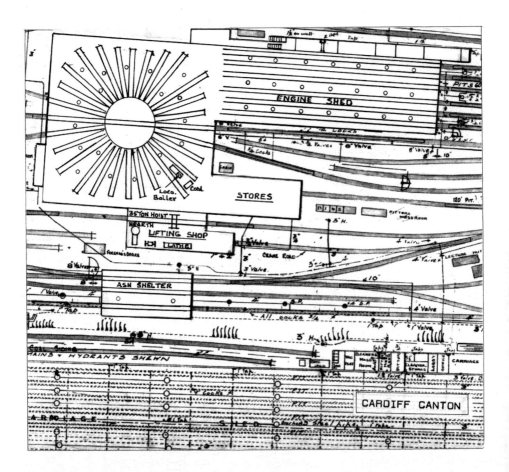

Aberdare (Newport Division)

Locomotives entering the yard proceed into a spur and make a reverse movement in order to gain access to the ash-dropping and coaling road. Coaling is effected by means of ½-ton-capacity coal tubs propelled across the coaling platform, which is 11ft 6in above the coaling road. This height is increased to 14ft 0in by means of an electrically operated lift built at the tip.

There are eight wagons of ash loaded weekly and the coal consumption approximates 490 tons per week.

The shed is of the single-unit turntable type, and from the table, which is 65ft in diameter, radiate twenty-eight pit roads of varying lengths, twenty-seven of which are used for stabling.

A boiler is positioned in the shed to supply steam for hot water boiler-washing.

A repair shop at the front of the loco shed contains two pit roads, and is equipped with a 35-ton overhead crane with a rope drive, together with smithing and machining facilities, etc.

The water supply for loco purposes is obtained from the River Cynon, water gravitating to a well near the loco shed, from whence it is pumped to a 74,250-gallon storage tank over the coal stage. An independent supply for drinking is provided.

Total number of engines allocated – 52:

2-8-0	6
2-8-2T	3
2-8-0T	11
0-6-2T	10
0-6-0T	22

Staff:

Supervisors	34
Clerical	7
Drivers	105
Firemen	103
Cleaners	32
Shed Grades	52
Fitters & Mates	16
Boilersmiths & Mates	8*
In Shop Fitters & Mates	11*

* Includes Chargeman

Summary of work performed:

Local passenger and freight working with tank engines over Vale of Neath line, also valley lines to Pontypridd, etc. Coal trains to Severn Tunnel Junction, Salisbury, etc. worked by heavy freight engines.

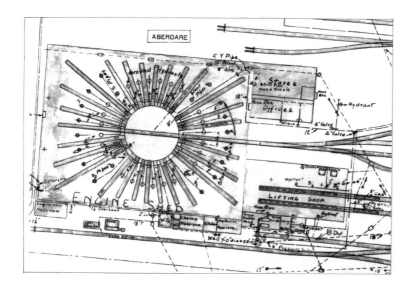

Cardiff (East Dock) Depot (Cardiff Valleys Division)

On entering the yard, locomotives are cleaned of ashes at the pit on the road leading to the coal stage, preparatory to being coaled. The coal stage, which is single sided, has a platform 13ft above rail level of loco road. Wheeled coal tubs of ½-ton capacity are used on the stage. Six wagons of ashes are loaded each week and coal consumption amounts to 387 tons per week.

The loco shed contains eight pit roads, all of which terminate inside.

Steam for use in connection with hot water boiler washing is obtained from a boiler house adjoining the shed, which contains two boilers.

For turning, a table 55ft in diameter is located near the shed,

A repair shop, also adjoining the loco shed, is of the one-road type and is provided with 35-ton electric engine hoist, together with machining and smithing facilities.

The water for loco purposes is drawn from a 74,250-gallon-capacity storage tank, built over the coal stage, which is supplied with softened water from the Crwys water softener situated north of Cardiff Queen Street station.

Total number of engines allocated – 65:		**Staff:**	
0-6-0T	45	Supervisors	3
0-6-2T	20	Clerical	5
		Drivers	110
		Firemen	95
		Cleaners	16
		Shed Grades	39
		Fitters & Mates	25
		Boilersmiths & Mates	5

Summary of work performed:

Coal trains – Rhymney Valley etc. Docks shunting engines.

Cardiff (Cathays) depot (Cardiff Valleys Division)

Locomotives enter the yard on the coaling road, ashes being dropped adjacent to and in the ash pit. The single-sided coal stage platform, 13ft above pit rail level, has three tiping points, wheeled coal tubs of ½-ton capacity being used for coaling. Locomotives, after coaling, proceed to shed or to the outgoing pit road. Ashes loaded amount to seven wagons per week and coal consumption in 589 tons weekly.

The main servicing portion of the shed contains five long dead-end roads, on each of which are two pits.

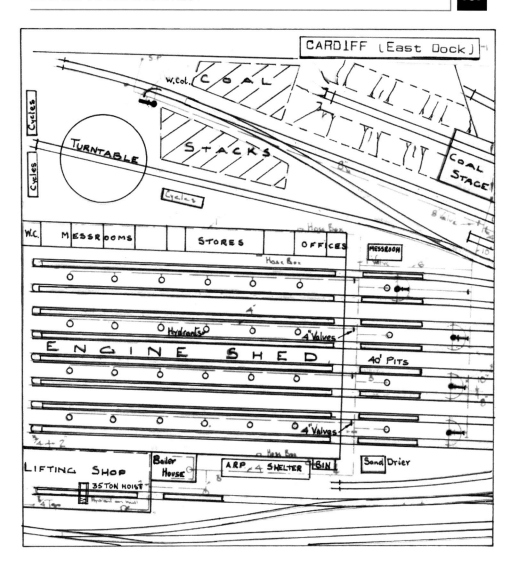

For turning purposes a 55ft-diameter turntable is provided.

Steam for combining with cold water to provide hot water for boiler washing is drawn from a boiler house containg two boilers, situated at the rear of the loco shed.

Machine and smiths shops etc. are attached to the rear of the loco shed. Repairing facilities also include a 35-ton engine hoist, electrically operated.

A storage tank near the turntable with a capacity of 31,000 gallons supplies water for all loco purposes, and is fed by means of a connection and pipeline from the corporation service, drinking water connections being taken off the pipeline before it reaches the tank.

Total number of engines allocated – 52:		**Staff**		**Sub-depots:**	
0-6-2T	41	Supervisors	4	Radyr – 27 engines:	
0-6-0T	8	Clerical	6	2-8-2T	2
0-4-2T	3	Drivers	112	0-6-2T	24
		Firemen	95	2-4-0T	1
		Cleaners	23	One 55ft-diameter	
		Shed Grades	46	turntable.	
		Fitters & Mates	29		
		Boilersmiths & Mates	5		

Summary of work performed

Coal trains – Rhymney Valley, Taff Vale section, etc. Local passenger and auto services.

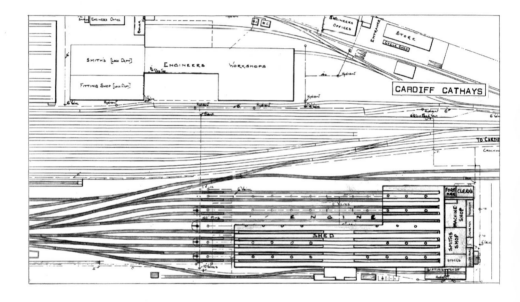

Danygraig Depot (Neath Division)

Locomotives arriving on the depot are first cleaned of ashes on the coaling road, then coaled at the elevated platform-type coal stage, the height of the platform being 11ft above coaling road rail level. Wheeled ½-ton-capacity coal tubs are used on the platform. The make of ash is two wagons per week and 172 tons of coal are loaded weekly.

The loco shed has four roads, two of which are extended through the rear of the shed and the other two of which are a little over half the length of the shed.

There is no turntable at this depot.

Steam for hot water boiler-washing purposes is drawn from a stationary boiler.

The repair shop adjoining the loco shed has three roads and is equipped with a 30-ton overhead crane which is rope driven off a shafting. Smithing and machining facilities are also provided.

The water supply is taken from the Neath RDC mains and the storage tank is of 46,700 gallons' capacity.

Total number of engines allocated – 30:

2-8-0T	1
0-6-0T	19
0-4-T	10

Staff:

Supervisors	1
Clerical	4
Drivers	72
Firemen	66
Cleaners	10
Shed Grades	19
Fitters & Mates	23
Boilersmiths & Mates	2

Summary of work performed:

Dock shunting and freight trip working in Swansea area.

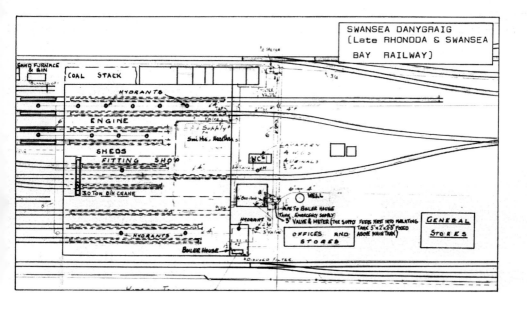

SWANSEA DANYGRAIG
(Late RHONDDA & SWANSEA
BAY RAILWAY)

Llanelly Depot (Neath Division)

Locomotives entering the yard proceed to one or the other side of a two-sided elevated platform coaling stage, according to their type. Ashes are dropped from locomotives on to the ash flats before coaling takes place. The coaling platforms, on which are propelled ½-ton-capacity tipping coal tubs, are 13ft above the loco road rail level. There are eight wagons of ash and 600 tons of coal loaded each week.

The loco shed is of the twin-unit turntable type, containing two 65ft-diamater manually operated tables, interconnected. These tables are located off-centre in their respective sheds, thus enabling radiating pit roads of varying lengths to be built to cater for locomotives of different lengths.

Hot water boiler-washing facilities exist at all shed roads, the steam being drawn from two boilers located at the front of the repair shop.

The repair shop adjoins the loco shed and has one pit road. It is equipped with a 35-ton loco hoist, which can be hand-operated or driven by belting off steam-engine-driven shafting. Machining and smithing arrangements are also provided.

The water provision is a metered supply from the town's industrial water system to a 180,000-gallon water tank over the coal stage, which supplies the columns, hydrants, etc. Drinking water is taken through a separate metered connection from the town's domestic mains.

A loco oil-fuelling plant exists near the repair shop, consisting of three horizontal storage tanks and pump house, etc. At present this is on a 'care and maintenance' basis.

Total number of engines allocated – 68

4-6-0	5
2-8-0	3
2-6-0	4
2-8-2T	3
2-8-0T	11
0-6-0T	39
0-6-2T	3

Staff

Supervisors	5
Clerical	7
Drivers	139
Firemen	138
Cleaners	18
Shed Grades	51
Fitters & Mates	34
Boilersmiths & Mates	7

Subdepots:

Patyffnon – 13 engines:

2-8-0T	4
0-6-0T	9

Burry Port – 7 engines

0-6-0T	7

one 65ft turntable.

Summary of work performed:

Main-line and local freight services. Three passenger turns only to Llandovery etc.

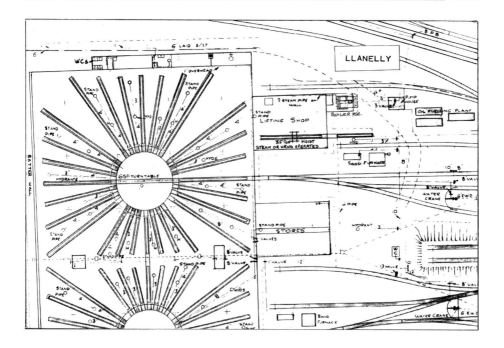

Duffryn Yard Depot (Neath Division)

On entering the yard, locomotives proceed direct to the coaling road where ashes are unloaded to the ash flat from whence they are manually loaded into wagons standing on the adjacent siding. Coaling is effected from an elevated coaling platform 13ft above the coaling road rail. Coal tubs of ½-ton capacity are used on the platforms. The average weekly make of ash is seven wagons, and the coal consumption is 544 tons per week.

For turning locomotives, a 45ft turntable, manually operated, is sited off the rear of the shed, from which locos return to a six-road dead-end shed.

Hot water boiler washing facilities exist, steam for this purpose being drawn from an adjacent boiler house having one boiler.

The repair shop contains one pit road and is equipped with a 35-ton hoist that can be hand- or belt-driven. Machining facilities are also installed.

The water supply for locomotives is drawn from a 19,400-gallon storage tank situated at the rear of the sheds, this tank supplying the columns and boiler washing mains. The tank is normally fed by means of a 6in metered supply from the council main, with a drinking and domestic supply taken from the feed main before it reaches the tank. When this supply fails, through shortage of town water, the tank is fed by water pumped from a well, which is supplied with river water by gravitation.

Total number of engines allocated – 55:

2-8-0T	5
2-6-2T	1
0-6-2T	16
0-6-0T	33

Staff:

Supervisors	3
Clerical	8
Drivers	145
Firemen	148
Cleaners	18
Shed Grades	46
Fitters & Mates	20
Boilersmiths & Mates	7

Summary of work performed:

Local freight and coal trains with tank engines. Shunting at Port Talbot Docks. Two local passenger turns – workmen's services, etc.

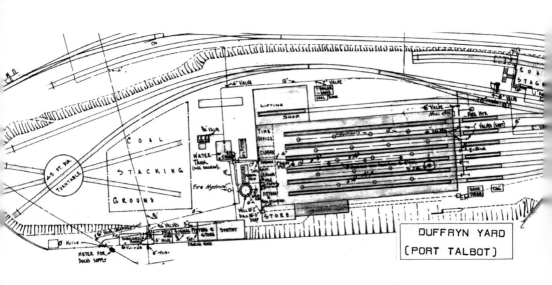

DUFFRYN YARD
(PORT TALBOT)

2

Steam Locomotive Builders and Repairers Associated with the GWR and its Constituent Companies

The birth of the Great Western Railway, as with all other railway companies of the period, included a major requirement: the 'motive power' source.

The development of the first locomotives had been to power the early tramroads and plateways for comparatively short journeys to the nearest canal with products from the mines and quarries, but the carriage of passengers opened up a completely new concept of 'railways'. Thus the makers of these locomotives, by the time of Stephenson's 'Planet' design, were the only experienced manufacturers available and the Planet design had proved itself.

The designs available in the first railway boom were thus very similar in their general principles of construction, so the first orders went to the established manufacturers, generally following the designs shown by the drawings illustrating these notes. Many of the growing number of new railway companies, as they developed, placed orders with several established makers with no, or at least very little, thought of 'maintenance' and 'standardisation', thus introducing further problems for themselves. Whilst designs had become established, trust Brunel to put a spanner in the works with specifications and designs that were completely alien to anything anyone had seen before, being far bigger because of the gauge of track, adding to manufacturing complications. Later the designs of Thomas Crampton had a similar effect, but at least they were standard gauge and they worked well.

The idea of making their own rolling stock was thus non-existent with most companies, or at best a dream for the future, and very few had realised the need for workshops to maintain stock, let alone make their own! We have seen in the previous pages of this book how the workshops were developed, with a selected few actually designing and making their own locomotives, and with the continual expansion of the GWR, maintenance of the rolling stock of the absorbed companies, so varied in design and makers, fell to the Great Western.

Whilst some of the absorbed companies had *built* their own locomotives, it did not follow that they *made* their own locomotives. A number of the railway companies had incomplete facilities; for example, the workshops had no ferrous or non-ferrous foundries and such requirements were bought-in from other sources, so, for example, a cylinder block could be machined but could not have been cast at their workshop.

Therefore, as the Great Western expanded, maintenance of stock from the absorbed companies (some had only one or two locomotives) became more and more complicated. Over the years, as the locos came in for servicing, various components were changed for as many 'standard' Great Western fittings as could be adapted. These often included complete boilers, saddle tanks changed to pannier tanks, and many of the smaller fittings.

There now follows a representative list of locomotive manufacturing companies from which the constituent companies, including on occasions the Great Western itself, obtained their rolling stock. Included are thumbnail sketches of the story of some of the main manufacturers supplying the railway companies that became part and parcel of the Great Western as it developed.

Who built the first Great Western locomotives?

In the formative years of the steam locomotive, the contractor, in modern language 'had it made'. The customer, with a backing of money to construct a railway subscribed by entrepreneurs and businessmen, was firmly in the hands of the contractor. He, the customer, with either vague or positive ideas about the locomotives required depending on experience, specified what he wanted and then sat back waiting for the contract to be completed and the locomotive delivered. The effectiveness of the locomotive depended on the design and the workmanship of the contractor, which were often both in his hands and certainly depending on his experience.

What if he, the customer, did not like what he received? He could send them or it back, but there were problems. A locomotive was usually delivered in part-assembled 'kit' form by canal, river, sea and then the shortest overland road route possible. Having waited some time for the steam power source of his railway, the customer could be forgiven for showing some reluctance to send his loco or locos back! We have earlier examined the problems that faced Brunel and Gooch when their first locomotives were received, and the work that was undertaken to get the engines working with a reasonable degree of success.

The contractor was very fortunate in that his sole concern was with making, and possibly designing to a specification, a steam locomotive that would run on someone else's railway, and indeed, this applied to the end of steam and beyond. Not for him was the design of the track and buildings, and the financial control and organisation for commercial traffic over iron rails.

Let us now have a brief look at the contract firms that were to supply the first locomotives to the GWR. It is safe to say that, generally, equipment and methods were similar in such firms, as they were all making basically similar products. The skills of the staff compared generally one with another. Of the firms concerned, their futures were very varied, and they were working concerns long before the Great Western's Swindon Works was built.

At the time of its conception, and selection of the site for its construction, there is an interesting speculation that may be made concerning Swindon, or indeed any loco works. It is and indeed was an accepted fact that locomotives need to be maintained. It is a completely different type of requirement to actually *make* locomotives. To tie the construction of a locomotive fleet to the railway company that is concerned with its commercial use requires very careful thought. Would it be done today? Few of the GWR's later constituent companies did so even in that entrepreneur age.

It is, for example, comparatively straightforward to, say, bore out a cylinder casting or re-bush a connecting rod, but there is a vastly different requirement in terms of facilities and indeed range of skills, to actually make the items from scratch. A few of the early railway companies set up their own workshops for manufacture, due often to the conditions of 'communication' prevailing, governed by financial backing, labour availability and existing transport means. The slow canals and appalling roads made it a desirable achievement to be self supporting, relying only on raw materials being delivered by the existing methods. As the rail networks spread, the isolation of such works diminished in the mesh of communicating rail tracks, leading to improved communication generally.

Those who were purely manufacturers, such as the examples following, and who made some of the first Great Western engines, became very worried over the business rivalry potential that they could foresee. With the spread of railway companies with the facilities to build locomotives for themselves, it was a very short step, if indeed a step at all, for such companies to enter the open market in competition with the companies solely manufacturing locomotives.

The potential of such competition was too much, and in 1876 the manufacturers banded together in an attempt to stop railway companies using their own facilities for the commercial construction of steam locomotives. From the first flush of enthusiasm for making their own motive power, and of course not aware of the later restrictions, was it such a good idea to make your own rolling stock? When looked at coolly, it is a tremendous undertaking. How many bus companies do you know that makes their own buses?

It was probably a product of the entrepreneurial age from which it stemmed, and it is very doubtful, given similar circumstances today, if the railway companies would again invest in such proportion to make their own railway stock. It was increasingly questionable, when such building was going on, whether it was cheaper in the long run to buy outside or to make your own. Current events are showing that it is cheaper to buy outside, and although 'costing' systems were much simpler in the early days, it is likely that, even then, it was cheaper to 'contract out'.

The 1968 Transport Act allowed railway workshops to tender for outside work, thus ending the restrictions of the earlier Act, and allowing an open door to the commercial world outside, but the market openings for the steam locomotives that had made the works famous had really gone. The general engineering and fabrication orders that *were* available were already in a market for which facilities existed elsewhere. The railway shops, in terms of machinery, organisation, staffing and, most importantly, in pricing and delivery dates, were not streamlined enough to compete.

For twenty years the Swindon Works staggered on, attempting to live in the commercial world, the smaller workshops spread over the region disappearing one by one under the iron ball of the demolition contractors.

All of the lesser works have gone, and a few hundred yards from where this is being written, the demolition of the world-famous A shop complex at Swindon was witnessed. In the dust, rubble, flickering fires and falling walls, 'Finis' was being written on the last page of Swindon's practical association with locomotives, and indeed railway history.

However, to return to the beginning, there follows an outline of those contractors who supplied the first locomotives to the Great Western Railway. From the following may be assessed the experience of the first contractors as they faced the first orders from a small, odd railway, one which did not, at the time, go anywhere and which in any case was to a strange wide track gauge.

This same track gauge requirement must also have caused problems in the workshops of the contractors: 4ft 8½in was the usual, up to 5ft 6in was known, but 7ft probably meant that the locos didn't really 'fit' anywhere or anything in the workshops!

The drawings included in this section illustrate locomotives of varying design and for other railway companies that were on the books of some of the manufacturers who received the first and some the follow-up orders from Brunel and Gooch. They serve to show the design progress and the standards which obtained at the time when Brunel first issued his difficult

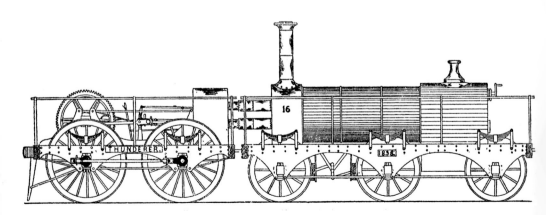

Great Western railway 'Thunderer', built by R.& W. Hawthorn of Newcastle.

specification for the locomotives required for the Great Western Railway, and later, in the period of orders placed by Gooch.

At the time of Brunel's first orders, designs had progressed to the state where, although experimentation continued, certain set features had emerged. For example, the boiler with its stayed structure of the firebox, the position of tubes and their general diameters and smokebox requirements were established. Certain features of valve-gear design and 'events' being more clearly understood, the evolving gear designs were to develop into the half dozen or so that were to dominate locomotive design until the end of official steam. At the period in question, however, it must be appreciated that whilst the design principles remained the same, locomotives for broad gauge were considerably bigger than their standard- or narrow-gauge equivalents.

List of representative locomotive builders

Brunel's first orders:

1.	Mather, Dixon & Co.	1826–43
2.	Messrs Hawthorn	1817 to date
3.	Charles Tayleur & Co.	1830 to date
4.	Robert Stephenson Co.	1823 to date
5.	The Haigh Foundry	1810

Later orders placed by Gooch:

1.	Jones, Turner & Evans	1837
2.	Fenton, Murray & Jackson	1795–1843
3.	Nasmyth, Gaskell & Co.	1836–1939
4.	Sharp, Roberts & Co.	1828–1903
5.	R.B. Longridge	1785–1855
6.	Stothert & Slaughter	1821–1935
7.	G.J. Rennie	1824–90

Note: the first five show locomotives built for other Railways at a time and by the firms that constructed the first GWR locomotives to Brunel's specification. The following seven show other products of all seven firms, which built the Great Western's 'Firefly' Class *c.* 1840. All locomotives of this period, and since, were effectively developments of Messrs Stephenson's 'Patentee' design of 1833.

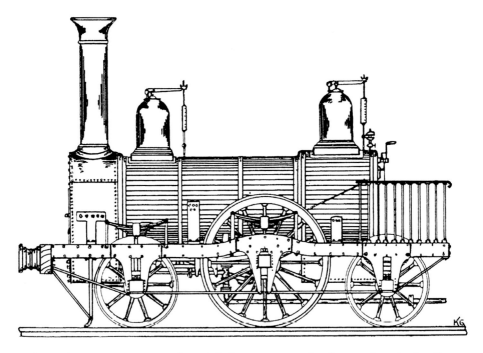

Mather, Dixon & Co., *c.* 1893. This 2-2-2 shows an example of a two-dome boiler. These were introduced at this time to overcome the problem of where to position the regulator – at or away from the steam collecting point, usually directly above the firebox.

Messrs R. & W. Hawthorn constructed this locomotive for the Newcastle & Carlisle Railway in 1835, for the opening of the line in that year. Wheels were 4ft in diameter and in the four-coupled formula.

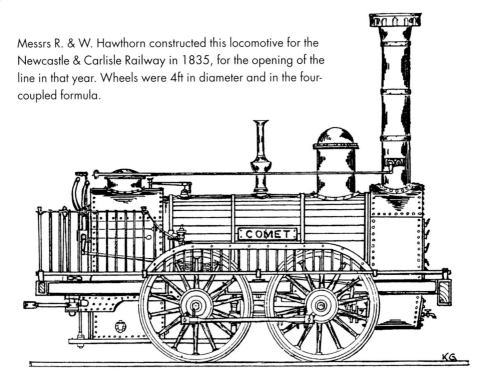

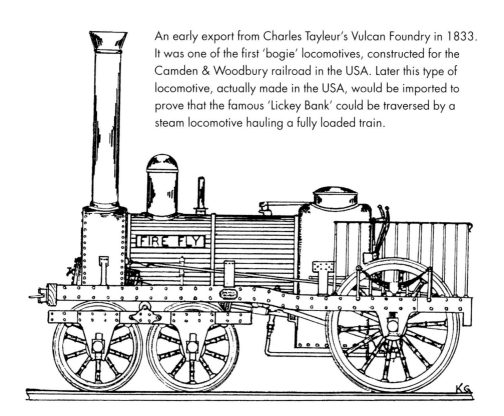

An early export from Charles Tayleur's Vulcan Foundry in 1833. It was one of the first 'bogie' locomotives, constructed for the Camden & Woodbury railroad in the USA. Later this type of locomotive, actually made in the USA, would be imported to prove that the famous 'Lickey Bank' could be traversed by a steam locomotive hauling a fully loaded train.

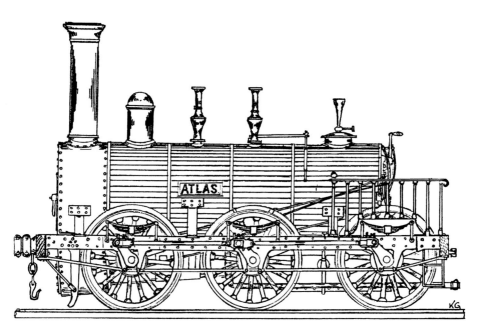

Atlas was constructed by Robert Stephenson Co. for the Leicester & Swannington Railway in 1834. The locomotive worked for about forty years had had been one of the first fitted with a steam trumpet, a forerunner of the warning whistle.

The Haigh Foundry, Wigan-built *Hector*, also built for the Leicester & Swannington Railway in 1838. A very powerful engine, it had been designed reputedly for a boiler pressure of 120lb – very high for the period.

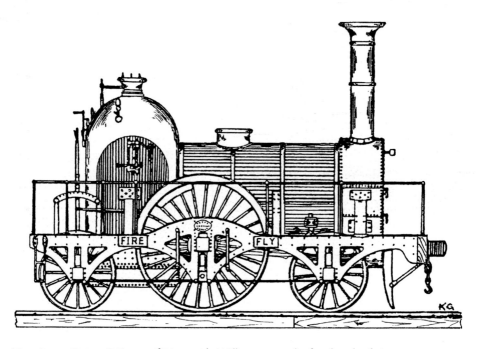

From Jones, Turner & Evans of Newton-le-Willows came the first bacth of sixty-two locomotives ordered by Daniel Gooch for the broad gauge Great Western. The 2-2-2 example *Fire Fly*, gave the class its name and ran for about thirty years until 1870.

This 2-2-0 was built in 1830 in the style of a Stephneson 'Planet', with 5ft driving wheels, by Messrs Fenton, Murray & Jackson.

Nasmyth, Gaskell & Co. built a batch of four of the first broad-gauge six-coupled engines owned by the Great Western, which were also unique in having outside sandwich frames. *Tityos* was delivered in 1842 and worked until 1870. The others in the batch had much the same lifespan.

A measure of standardisation was in existence by the 1830s, and Messrs Sharp, Roberts & Co. adopted this design of 2-2-2 as their standard passenger engine in 1837. Several hundred were built for many railway systems, and the format, to more powerful dimensions of cylinders and wheels, lasted about twenty years.

This old establishment firm constructed steam engines and locomotives for many years. R.B. Longridge and Co. locomotives were in use on many of the world's railways and included multiple designs, one of which is the Robert Stephenson 'long boiler' type. An 1843 goods version is depicted here.

Avalanche is a somewhat mysterious locomotive, built for the broad-gauge Great Western in 1846 by Stothert & Slaughter. One of a kind, it started life as a tender engine, but, seemingly to increase adhesion, was rapidly converted to a saddle tank. It is listed in this form as a 'banker' at Box Tunnel. It ceased this duty in 1865.

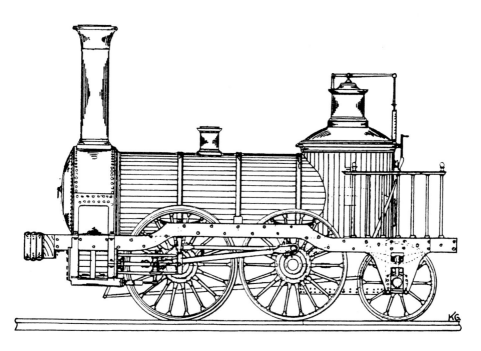

G.J. Rennie was one of the latecomers into the locomotive manufacturing business, but introduced several unique features. These included the first use of horizontal cylinders working directly on the driving wheel crank pins, and an oval (in plan) firebox. The drawing shows the 1838 design for the London & Croydon Railway.

The unsteadiness of the four-wheeled goods engine prompted Robert Stephenson to add another pair of wheels at the firebox end. This addition, in 1833, so improved the riding quality that the six-wheel passenger design *Patentee* set the trend towards the modern locomotive.

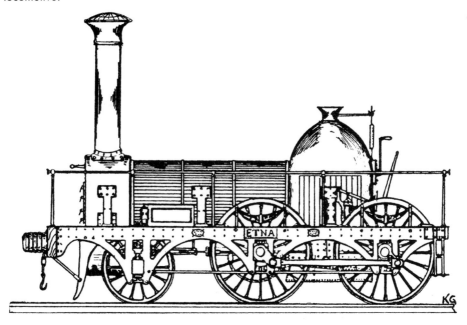

Delivered in 1841, *Etna* was one of a class of the Great Western's first goods engines and worked until 1866. Included in a batch of eighteen, it was one of three built by Messrs Fenton, Murray & Jackson.

Hurricane, built by R. & W. Hawthorn of Newcastle for the GWR.

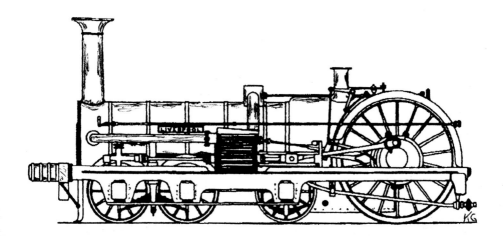

Crampton Locomotive *Liverpool*, LNWR 1848.

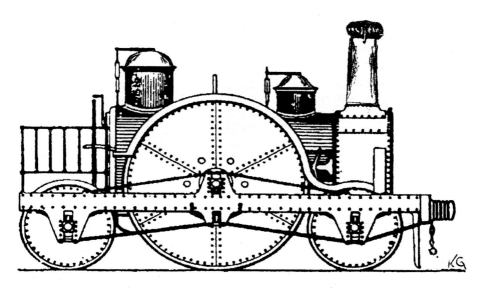

Ajax, built by Mather Dixon & Co. in 1838 for the GWR.

Mather, Dixon & Co. 1826–43

Among the first batch of contractors and makers of the 10ft-diameter plate-wheeled *Ajax* and *Mars* (with difficulties previously outlined) was Mather, Dixon & Co. of Bath Street Foundry, Liverpool. As with many of the early locomotive-building firms, Mather, Dixon had started in 1826 with contracts for marine and stationary engines, and as soon as the locomotive engine was shown to be viable, decided to expand to include the new enterprise of locomotive building.

The expansion required that they should first obtain a steam loco for their own use for shunting (and probably to gain some knowledge of design and handling), so a small 0-4-0 tank was built at the works the year after opening. Lifting was shown to be a problem, so two cranes followed and then for internal movement in the shop a steam traversing table, again to their own design, was made and installed, and they then felt ready to receive orders.

Their first orders were to push them directly into a very early export market for steam locomotives. The firm of Edward Bury & Co., also of Liverpool (and established for several years before Mather, Dixon) had an overflowing order book and so an order for three of Bury's bar frame 0-4-0 locomotives was subcontracted. These were from a larger order of Bury's for the Petersburg Railroad in America, and were shipped out early in the 1830s. Mather, Dixon was now established in the loco-building business, and the orders flowed in. Liverpool Docks, wishing to use a local firm with capacity, had four tank engines built in 1834, followed by steam cranes for Birkenhead Docks.

Other small engines were built for collieries, and the export orders continued with a batch of three for Russia. In the mid 1830s, when the six-wheeled loco appeared, Mather, Dixon decided to attempt a 'standardisation' in the vogue. Thus were prepared designs for four classes of the six-wheeler, the variations of 0-6-0, 0-4-2, 2-4-0, and 2-2-2, one of each being built as showroom exhibits for potential customers – so far so good.

More of the 0-4-0 Bury types were also built for the London & Birmingham Railway, and the Liverpool and Manchester had 2-2-2 and 0-4-2s constructed in 1836–37. Then along came Brunel's order, with specifications! With the problems previously outlined, it must in fairness be said that the experience of Mather, Dixon was not at fault when viewed in the context of the period in which the events occurred. They were probably a little overpowered by the requirements of the order and Brunel's reputation as an engineer. They were also probably very glad to see the order disappear toward the docks, away from their works, for final shipment to the Great Western.

Several more 'conventional' locos followed, including a 6ft single 2-2-2 for the Tsarskoe Selo Railway in Russia. Business was good, and the firm moved premises in 1839, starting with a batch production of fifteen locos of 2-2-2 format. These were sold in twos and threes to the burgeoning railway systems in the British boom years, as well as two to the Paris–Orleans Railway. The French were soon to become entranced with the Crampton designs – designs which did not find too much favour in their country of origin.

Others had leapt on to the locomotive-building bandwagon in those boom years and the early 1840s saw a drop in orders. This was to such an effect that for two or three years only replacement boilers were built and the showroom examples disposed of through an agent. In

1842, a batch of five 2-2-2s was built along with a solitary 2-4-0, without orders and with again a speculative, last-ditch effort to stay in business. With two unfinished 0-6-0s coupled in the shops, Mather, Dixon ceased trading in 1843.

With a total output of seventy-five engines to its credit, Mather, Dixon went out of business in the year the brand new works at Swindon started on its long, successful and expansive career.

Messrs R. & W. Hawthorn – 1817 to date

To commence a very long history, latterly combines in the history of another famous company, the firm of the brothers R. & W. Hawthorn opened for business in 1817. As with others of the early years, stationary engines started off the production side followed by a marine application. The progress into the steam locomotive world came naturally once the potential was seen, and, as with Mather, Dixon & Co., a venture into the export business started the ball rolling. A 2-2-2 was built for Austria in 1831, a design with condensing facilities, and then a batch of six ordered for the Stockton & Darlington Railway. They were later to expand the export side with locos for Austria, Germany, Sweden, Denmark, India, Africa, Australia and South America, some of which were of Crampton design, but at the moment were still feeling their way.

The S & D Railway six were in the historical mould of vertical cylinders driving a shaft which connected to the front coupled wheels, and formed the nucleus of the 'Majestic' and 'Wilberforce' classes, all 0-6-0 format. A 0-4-0 in the same vertical-cylinder format was also built a little later for the same railway in the late 1830s. A special valve gear had been designed for some of the earlier designs, using a swivelling block in the connecting rod and rocking arm arrangement, but the Howe link changed all that in the 1840s. The latter 0-4-0, named *Swift*, had a wheel-less axle, or jack shaft, between the two pairs of wheels, and to which eccentrics were fitted, the boiler itself carrying the motion link fulcrums.

It was to this firm then that Brunel's initial order for two locomotives was presented. It is, as a speculation, quite possible that the firm was a little perplexed over the nature of the order. First the gauge but also other requirements of Brunel, which must have been specified, were certainly out of the ordinary for the period. The answer was thought to be the application of T.E. Harrison's patent, of putting the boiler on one set of wheels with the 'engine' on another set, both sets flexibly connected, and spreading the overall weight. It was also easier to mount a big boiler without the complication of the 10ft wheels and related crank axle clearance.

Again to conform to requirements, the 10ft wheel rolled into view, with the same lack of success as the Mather, Dixon 10-footer. So *Hurricane* blew itself out, and its fellow locomotive *Thunderer* followed like a wet squib, the latter's 6ft drivers and associated gearing giving the equivalent of an 18ft-diameter wheel. Neither was a success, and a short life followed.

This was an experience the Hawthorn brothers did not repeat, although it was a very bold attempt to conquer the unusual by applying the unusual. Apart from flexible coupling difficulties from boiler to engine, adhesion of the wheels was not, and could not, be successful.

The locomotives have been compared with, and called, the forerunners of the Beyer Garrets and the like. In principle this is probably correct, but with the modern design, the 'driving' mechanisms are under the two ends, with the boiler in the centre, giving maximum adhesion to the driving wheels. With the *Thunderer* and *Hurricane*, the only actual driver wheels were the 10ft or 6ft geared, set in the centre of the arrangement, there being no power adhesion from any of the other wheels.

Irrespective of this experimental 'hiccup', the firm went from strength to strength, building a very wide range of locomotives to conventional (as it developed) design and also Crampton types for export. They were still innovative and open-minded, and built specialist locomotives as well. Later in the century they were to build very distinctive crane engines, (small locos with a steam-powered crane built in to the design). Industrial locomotives of all designs were made, including 'fireless' designs for use in dangerously inflammable works sites. These latter designs were simply a combined water and steam receptacle, which could be topped up from tanks outside the danger zone. The high-pressure steam and water combined to produce lower-pressure steam for the short runs within the factory complex, with no smoke or fire being anywhere near the inflammable products.

Production of all types continued, and in 1906 a 'Railmotor' design was supplied to the Port Talbot Railway. This 77ft-long combined coach and engine was the largest of the type built, being an 0-6-0 power unit with 3ft-diameter wheels and 12in × 16in outside cylinders.

Two thousand, six hundred and eleven steam locomotives were built, covering several moves of premises and expansions of the firm, which had become Hawthorn Leslie & Co. in 1884 on merger with a shipbuilder. In 1937, the locomotive portion was purchased by R. Stephenson Company, becoming R. Stephenson & Hawthorn Ltd and at the time of writing is still going strong – albeit in combination with Charles Tayleur & Co. from 1944, and all reformed under the mantle of English Electric Co. from 1955.

Charles Tayleur & Company – 1830–1955 (and to date)

Lancashire, 1830, and Charles Tayleur, a director of the Liverpool & Manchester Railway, with an eye to potential business, went into partnership with Robert Stephenson, after a year or two sorting out the pros and cons of the locomotive construction business. Locos and items for his company's railway could thus be made almost on site, without the transportation problems from other more distant makers.

Starting with a couple of conventional 0-4-0s each to the Warrington & Newton Railway and the North Union Railway, export 4-2-0s to America followed in 1835 and were reputedly the first bogie locos built in Britain. The locos were to the tried Stephenson designs and orders followed for Austria, America, France, Belgium and Russia. The railway fever had spread. With the later development of the Stephenson long-boiler type, many were built through the 1840s, the usual 0-4-0, 0-4-2 and 2-2-2 format, and the order books remained full.

Also in the 1840s, the name of the firm changed to The Vulcan Foundry Co., and the association with Robert Stephenson had faded out, for the time anyway.

By the time of Brunel's order, however, Tayleur & Co. had had considerable experience in the building of steam locomotives, although eyebrows would possibly have been raised on receipt and scrutiny of Brunel's requirements. Boiler pressures of the period were about 50–55lb per square inch, and the required 2-2-2 wheel arrangement for the six locos ordered included a design necessity for an 8ft-diameter driver pair. In common with other makers, Tayleur had run into the same problem of large wheel diameter.

With massive wheels and comparatively small boilers feeding minuscule cylinders of 12 × 16in for the first three and 14 × 16in for the second three of the order, the locos must have had severe lung trouble, gasping for breath when pushing themselves along, let alone trying to haul a fast train! Out of the complete order, with all their problems, they were still reputedly the best of a very suspect lot and were subjected to other work when delivered, in the attempt to improve performance.

Locomotives were built by the firm, again within the accepted conventions over the ensuing years, for almost every country where the steam loco ran.

One very longstanding association was that of constructing locomotives for India, commencing just after the turn of the half-century with eight 2-4-0s for the Great Indian Peninsula Railway. The 'Fairlee' patent locos are among some prominent designs for both home use and export, being constructed from 1872 for such diverse companies as the 3ft 6in gauge Dunedin and Port Chalmers Railway and the 2ft 6in gauge of the Peruvian Government tracks. A 'plate' railway loco was supplied to the Tredegar Iron Works 2ft 11¼in gauge track as well as 'standard-gauge' locos for the Midland Railway during the 1870s.

In 1898 the firm became Vulcan Foundry Ltd, and world orders were dominated by those from India and South America. An extensive range of locomotives was produced, from small crane tanks to 4-8-4s for the Chinese National Railway, with almost every wheel arrangement in the book!

The growth of foreign manufacturing facilities, cut-throat competition and the coming of the end of steam meant a complete rethink in terms of the diesel and the electric loco.

A total of 6,210 steam locos of various designs and gauges were constructed during the lifetime of the firm, which officially ended early in 1944 when it merged with its previous business rivals Robert Stephenson & Hawthorn. A restructuring in 1955 brought all together under the umbrella of the English Electric Group, in which it continues.

Robert Stephenson Co. – 1823–1955 (to date)

A famous father with a famous son is not unique in history, but the name of George Stephenson and his son Robert are among those remembered by all schoolboys.

From the earliest attempts to mechanise internal colliery transport, George Stephenson's record of steam engine construction had reached fifty-five, of which sixteen were of the locomotive type, the earliest being for the Killingworth Colliery and built in 1814. Thus the year before Wellington and Blucher chased Napoleon off the field of Waterloo, and two years after Napoleon's debacle at Moscow, the hiss of motive steam power was in the air. Rather interestingly, this first loco was named *Blucher*.

All were of the vertical-cylinder variety, and with the exception of one 0-6-0 were of the 0-4-0 wheel designation. To Stephenson the potential was obvious, and in 1823 a four-man partnership comprising George, his son Robert, Edward Pearce and Micheal Longridge, who had his own engineering works, established the first steam locomotive manufactory in the world. The original 8-acre site, a very progressive size after the usual utilisation of colliery facilities for locomotive building, was established at Forth Street, Newcastle upon Tyne. For this enterprise most of the engineering facilities were, of necessity, home-made at the works from equally home-made designs.

We can picture the usual quite extensive blacksmith facilities and the foundry, along with an embryo machine shop. It was only a few years after Maudsley had given us the table engine (where the crank pin was driven by rod from the cross head and had dispensed with Watt's beam), and had also experimented with and developed the lathe for screw-cutting in the modern sense. Maudsley had also introduced (in a move that would later influence Whitworth) a series of taps and dies for a 'standard' approach to screw threads, dependent on material diameter.

From the new works the famous locomotion No. 1 was produced, quickly followed by 0-4-0 and 0-6-0 designs for the Stockton and Darlington. American exports were also catered for, in the order for two different engines for two brand-new railways. The first was for a four-coupled loco with 4ft wheels and long-stroke 9in × 24in cylinders, destined for the Delaware & Hudson Railroad, and which safely reached its American tracks. The other, a 0-6-0 coupled for the Boston & Providence Railroad lies somewhere, new and unused, at the bottom of the Atlantic Ocean, the only bell ringing for it being the disaster bell at Lloyds, after its transporting vessel disappeared at sea.

Following the *Rocket*, whose story is too well known to repeat here, came *Invicta*, for the Canterbury & Whitstable Railway, the first real passenger locomotive. As with its rival firms of repute, R. Stephenson had to spread their orders by subcontracting so great was the demand at this period. Orders for America continued, again the 'bogie' type, which seemed to find such favour in that country, and all in all, R. Stephenson was probably the most highly experienced builder in the world. With various innovations to its credit, the long boiler, the inclusion of four eccentrics for the valve gear, which was improved upon, and later the 'link' motion to replace the gab, all pointed to innovation and development expertise.

The two very effective, for the period, locomotives *North Star* and *Morning Star* sold, almost by accident, to the troubled Great Western, and proved the effectiveness of the designs and workmanship from the Stephenson firm. Robert Stephenson was again involved indirectly in contest with the Great Western later in 1846 when the gauge controversy was raging. The Great Western, although deeply involved, were not directly in the contest with a Great Western-built engine, but the opposition to their entry was a long-boiler Stephenson 4-2-0.

This locomotive was for the York & North Midland 4ft 8½in gauge and was unnamed, known solely as 'A' in the contest. It had a Bury-type firebox and 15in × 24in cylinders fed from a low-centre-of-gravity boiler, and although it was outclassed completely by broad-gauge opposition, the narrow gauge itself was winning the war!

Locomotives continued to be built by Robert Stephenson for literally worldwide application, wherever railways existed and by as early as 1855 over 1,000 locomotives had been built. The orders continued to pour in and in 1902 bigger premises were sought. After a move of all facilities to Springfield, Darlington production continued apace until in 1937 the firm amalgamated with Messrs Hawthorn, having built about 4,200 locomotives of all designs for many countries.

The workload continued to flourish and a year later Kitson & Co. and Manning Wardle & Co. were absorbed into the new Stephenson & Hawthorn Co. In 1944, the old Tayleur-Stephenson contact was renewed after a period of about 110 years when the two firms' founder names became once more associated. The fireless loco remained in production and the last steam loco proper to be built was for Messrs Stewarts & Lloyds (steel manufacturers) in 1958. The old works of both Stephenson & Hawthorn, first loco builders, has now gone, but the companies are perpetuated within the English Electric Co. Ltd.

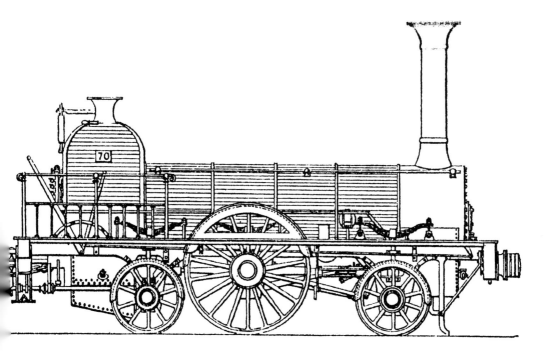

Stephenson's 'long boiler' locomotive.

The *North Star* as originally built by Messrs Robert Stephenson & Co. in 1837.

The Haigh Foundry, Wigan – 1810–56

The expansion of engineering in the early nineteenth century included the establishment in 1810 of the Haigh Foundry. In keeping with the growth of mining and iron making, the two facets, engineering and the basics of industry coal and iron production, were growing together, power winding and pumping machinery being in great demand. The later beckoning finger of the steam locomotive caused a new company to be formed in 1835 to include building the newfangled steam locomotive, under Mr W. Melling, works manager.

Among the first in the field, already mentioned, had been Edward Bury, and his overflowing order books had formed the start for several locomotive builders, orders being subcontracted to the new firms. The Haigh Foundry Co. was among the recipients of subcontracts from Bury and construction started on the Bury, almost a classic, 0-4-0 and 2-2-0 four-wheelers for which he is so well known. A couple of six-wheelers, an 0-4-2 for the Leicester & Swannington Railway and a later 0-6-0 of 17 tons followed. The second order came, probably due to the quick fulfilment of the first order literally weeks before the scheduled date of completion, and the order book rapidly filled.

The Brunel instructions were sent to the Haigh for two locomotives, the firm then well experienced having completed twenty-four locomotives of varying designs but mostly 2-2-0 and 2-2-2 for British and foreign companies, the latter the Paris & St Germain Railway. In 1838, the Brunel order was complete and *Viper* and *Snake* were wheeled out, reduced to transportable form and shipped off to the Great Western Railway. The firm was probably relieved to see the back of them.

In the general description of the locomotives, they appear to follow the usual design, but an addition was that of 'Melling's patent' in which the driving wheels were geared up in the ratio 3:2, (the John Melling of the patent was not connected to W. Melling, the Works Manager). The gearing was not successful and both locos were rebuilt later to a more conventional design.

A later indirect connection with the Great Western occurred in 1851–53 when the successor to Brunel, Daniel Gooch, designed four engines for the South Devon Railway. These were saddle tanks following the 'Corsair' Class, which had taken over after the failure of the atmospheric system. In keeping with the usual Gooch 'breed-em-tough' outlook for locomotive drivers and firemen, and relying on the milder climate of South Devon (hopefully), there was neither cab nor weatherboard on the design to protect the unfortunate pair! The four were named *Priam*, *Demon*, *Falcon* and *Orion*.

The Haigh Foundry built some of the different designs of the period. Thomas Crampton was now a designer in his own right and, although seemingly shunned in England, his designs found favour on the continent. The foundry built three locos to the Crampton patents, 7ft-diameter drivers with outside cylinders and valve gear, and after running in for a short period these were shipped to France. During the Crimean War, a pair of 0-8-0s were built for the government, specifically designed for 1-in-10 inclines and nominally to be the pullers of heavy guns. Outside cylinders, two pairs of flangeless wheels and an unusual circular but horizontal furnace (as opposed to the usual rectangular firebox) were features of the design.

A further pair of specials were built for Orrell Colliery near Wigan, these were 'rack railway' types and were probably on a subcontract basis. The 0-8-0s for the army in the Crimea were among the last orders completed. Business was getting slack and the lease on the premises was running out (it had been set in the first instance for twenty-one years), and renewal was not contemplated. With the completion of two further engines for Thomas Crampton, the doors of Haigh Foundry closed for the last time in 1856, a total of 114 locomotives of varying designs having been built.

Jones, Turner & Evans Viaduct Foundry, Newton-Le-Willows – 1837–1852

This was one of the new firms of the railway boom years, although quite efficient in spite of a seeming lack of experience. What may have been lacking in experience was apparently more than adequately covered by association with the well established firms of Edward Bury and of Robert Stephenson from whom substantial subcontract orders were forthcoming.

Variations of the six-wheel-format locomotive were made for the Midland Counties and the North Union Railways as well as 2-2-0s and 2-2-2s for the Great Western and London,

Brighton & Grand Junction lines. To add to this experience came the order from Daniel Gooch for six broad based 2-2-2s, the first of which off the list became the famous leader of the class, *Fire Fly*, always to be subsequently quoted and often illustrated in any GWR history in which it forms a significant factor.

The six locos of what became known as the Firefly Class were part of the order for sixty-two, which Gooch had spread in 1840 in little batches around seven of the various manufacturers of the day, some better and some lesser known but all producing effective versions of this updated copy of the Stephenson *North Star* on which the design had been based. Stephenson again features in further orders on the company, with 2-2-2s and 0-4-2s for export to Austria, including several to his long-boiler designs. Braithwaite of the Eastern Counties lines ordered 2-2-0s, and while these were under way in the workshops, the inflow of orders seemed to dry up.

A rather lean couple of years followed, repairs and spares just keeping the works moving up to the mid-1840s, when the name changed to Jones & Potts. Whilst the Jones of the name got on with keeping the workshops active, Mr Potts went out to get the orders in which he was very successfully employed. In 1845, Alexander Allen became involved with the firm and his designs were adopted, the standard format of outside cylinders and slotted frames giving a distinctive look to the firm's products.

Output and production appear to have been very effectively controlled and large orders for the Eastern Counties started with a first loco constructed between February and July 1845. The 4-2-0s followed, with long-boiler designs, and batches for the Scottish Railways were followed by Allen's outside-cylindered 'Crewe' type singles. An order for the London & Blackwall Railway, 2-2-2 well tanks, obtained in 1848, heralded another very slack period and the order book tailed right off. Orders failed to materialise and even Mr Potts could not drum up sufficient work. In 1852 there was no alternative but to close down, and the firm ceased trading.

This was not, however, to be the end of the story. The following year, having examined the site and the facilities, the London North Western Railway (LNWR) (one of the thorns in the side of the Great Western!) obtained a lease on the works. In 1860, full purchase negotiations were completed and the Earlestown Carriage & Wagon Works of the LNWR came into being. John Jones, one of the original partners, was still a locomotive man. He moved to Liverpool and completed another fifty or so engines, giving an overall total of 342, none of which are remembered to the extent of the Great Western's broad-gauge *Fire Fly*.

Early Great Western locomotives – the second contract phase

Having with extreme problems succeeded in getting the Great Western Railway on the rails, Messrs Brunel and Gooch still had no manufacturing facilities of their own. With a very mediocre locomotive fleet, some better than others and the Stephenson 'Stars' twinkling above the rest, a further design effort was required, this time based on the experience of the first contracted miscellany.

A first order was once again a Robert Stephenson's, perpetuating the most effective pair of the first batch with an order for ten more, delivered between 1839 and 1841. All had 7ft drivers and large domed fireboxes, differing in this respect from the two 'Stars' of the first batch. Other slight differences were apparent in smaller fittings and slight variations in cylinder sizes, but they were nevertheless 'Stars', with driving axles supported by six bearings.

Mention has already been made of the circumstances under which Gooch received instructions to design his own locomotives, and this he did using the best features of the first batch, mostly 'Star' features, in his designs. The Great Western, even at this early stage, did not do things by halves and orders were placed between 1840 and '42 for sixty-two express broad-gauge 2-2-2s, twenty-one smaller types for branch traffic and eighteen goods engines of 2-4-0 followed by four goods engines of 0-6-0 wheel format.

Orders were spread out among a number of manufacturers, and with the exception of Hawthorns, with an order for eight of the smaller branch locos, and probably with thoughts of the ineffective first batch, the orders went to new names in the construction field. Some of these were new names only in as much as they had not received Great Western orders before, although they had been in engineering for many years.

Fenton, Murray & Jackson – 1795–1843

The largest order for the express 2-2-2s went to Fenton, Murray & Jackson for a batch of twenty, the firm being long established in the engineering field and noted for expertise in stationary steam engines and early machine-tool manufacturing. Locomotives for colliery use had been built from the very early days, the first in 1812, and continuing with the Blenkinsop design of the rack locomotives, with traction depending on a toothed rail. These were built when the original partners were Fenton, Murray & Wood, and the firm, having built a very successful small batch of Blenkinsops, only possibly a half-dozen, then reverted to the stationary engine and machine-tool interest.

In 1831, the name of the firm changed to Fenton, Murray & Jackson and with it came a renewal of locomotive-building interest. The period was one of great demand and the order book filled rapidly. Apart from locos for British railway companies orders came from Russia, France, America and Belgium, previous known quality products assisting with the selling.

The loco output was mostly 2-2-2s with a scatter of other wheel formats, a requirement for three Great Western broad-gauge 2-4-0s starting off the Gooch order. These first three, made in 1840, were named *Hecla*, *Stromboli* and *Etna* and were followed by orders for twenty passenger 2-2-2s. Among this order, and completed in 1841, was *Ixion* which was to represent the broad gauge in the trials now under way, and which was to compete against the long-boiler Stephenson of the York & North Midland, the narrow-gauge (4ft 8½in) entrant. *Ixion* carried the day easily. A greater load pulled at a higher speed with great steadiness and steam reserves; in fact it won hands down.

It was to be the beginnings of the pyrrhic victory of the broad gauge because the trials and all the effort were really several years too late. The 4ft 8½in gauge had become, and was even then becoming, so well entrenched that continuing battles of the gauge war were coming up against so much narrow-gauge thinking that, in essence, that war was already lost, although prolonged for another half century.

The quality of workmanship of the Fenton, Murray & Wood, and latterly Fenton, Murray & Jackson, was maintained throughout the contract, producing, according to Gooch himself, the best locomotives of the complete order. Rather strangely, after such success, the firm suddenly folded in 1843, when it was continued for a very short time by what appears to be a first 'consortium' by workforce to continue on a profit-sharing basis.

The sudden demise leaves an interesting question. Did anything in the order for the broad-gauge locomotives catch the firm with a liquidity problem? It was quite a batch to deal with. Did they underquote or did a delay in payment from the Great Western cause their exit? Whatever the reason, the workers' consortium – a very tricky procedure – was not successful, due reputedly to malpractice, incompetence and downright dishonesty! It was rescued and taken over by a completely different partnership.

Locomotive building was never resumed and the new company ended its days in the 1890s as machine-tool manufacturers, at least keeping the one original and very successful product of the original firm to the end.

The products of the works were not confined to material items. During its long life it also fostered such well-known engineers as Richard Peacock, a co-partner in the Gorton Foundry of Beyer Peacock & Co., and well-known loco builders David Joy, of radial valve gear fame, and John Chester, the first loco superintendent of the LB&SC Railway, both received training at the Fenton, Murray & Jackson Round House Works.

Nasmyth, Gaskell & Co., Manchester – 1836–1939

Next on Gooch's list with an order for sixteen of the passenger 2-2-2s, the Bridgewater Foundry had started by making machine tools, stationary engines and other engineers' and military ordnance items. It had as its driving force the inventor of the steam hammer and, when the Gooch order for the sixteen locos arrived in 1842, had been involved in loco construction for only four years, with a total of thirty completed.

Following the order, a lull in construction, or orders, lasted until 1845. It appears that the main interest of the firm lay in general 'steam' products, with machine tools also an important item, but the steam hammer and associated piledriver, along with rolling mill equipment were in great demand.

It is with the steam piledriver that an indirect association with Robert Stephenson comes in. This adaption of the steam hammer was first used when Stephenson built the high bridge at Newcastle.

The company changed its name to James Nasmyth & Co. in 1850, and seven years later to Patricroft Iron Works. Eventually changing name again to Nasmyth, Gaskell & Co., the steam loco construction again came to the fore in the 1880s, the export side of the business overtaking almost all of the loco construction.

Orders came from many overseas countries, but with a reducing, and it must be said difficult, home market following the First World War, the firm closed its doors in 1939, having produced just over 1,500 steam locomotives in the ninety-one years of its existence. Its reputation for quality and its long association with the field of military ordnance caused it to be taken over as a Royal Ordnance factory in the year of closure, but its steam locomotive days had gone forever.

Sharp, Roberts & Co – 1828–1903 (and to 1962)

A pupil of the great Henry Maudesley, and destined to become one of several very distinguished engineers trained under his influence, Richard Roberts was joined by Thomas Sharp in a works manufacturing spinning machinery for the local cotton mills. Roberts' engineering skills were extended into the production of machine tools within the main categories of lathes, drilling machines, planers, punches and shears. The standards set by his tutor, Maudesley, had a knock-on effect in that precision machinery could also make precision machinery, which itself formed a continuing training sequence for further engineers. It was in this way that the market for such work really had no horizon once quality had become an established feature. This was the Roberts who had improved the lathe almost beyond recognition in 1817 with the four-step pulley, the 'back gear' and a 'self act' for automatic tool traverse independent of the 'lead screw'. The latter was a separately geared additional screw driven by a rather strange bevel gear arrangement, which nevertheless worked well.

To digress a little, a number of pupils into which Maudesley had instilled his engineering principles became famous in the engineering field, including Joseph Whitworth, who, among other achievements, pressed for the standardisation of the screw thread. Roberts, mentioned above, Nasmyth and Bodmer, the latter in the spinning industry, were all under the influence of Maudesley's precision engineering principles. Indeed, as well as his machine-tool achievements, Roberts, before his locomotive construction period, had developed Sam Crompton's Spinning Mule into a 2,400-spindle, semi-automatic monster, which required only one experienced spinner to supervise, with unskilled assistance.

In developing such machines, machine tools had to be devised to do the required work, and once built, immediately found a market. Stationary steam engines were built, and it was not long before the lure of mobile steam propelled the firm into its first locomotive order. This was for a 2-2-0 for the Liverpool & Manchester Railway, and was designed and built in 1833. Vertical cylinders, in the fashion of the time, were connected to crank pins in the wheels by levers and bell cranks, but after a series of breakdowns, with this and subsequently built engines, the more traditional (as it was to become) format was adopted. This was the 2-2-2 with inside cylinders and outside frames and introduced an almost standard Sharp Roberts with the combined dome and safety valve located at the front of the boiler close to the smokebox.

Such features were not evident on the order for ten which Gooch placed in 1842, the ten a part-order of the sixty-two Gooch-designed passenger 2-2-2s to the 7ft gauge. The 'standard' Sharp Roberts 2-2-2 was much more successful than the previous vertical-cylinder efforts, and although varying in some of the details, the many orders that were completed before 1860 totalled around 600 in the twenty years from introduction.

Roberts left the firm very early, in 1843, and the name changed to Sharp Brothers, changing again around the mid century into Sharp Stewart Co., on retirement of the elder brother. Order books remained full and locomotives got bigger. The interest in general engineering, foundry work and machine tools meant that extra space was required.

The usual problem arose when space was needed, in that there was nowhere in which to expand, so, finding the Clyde Locomotive Works of Glasgow was for sale, Sharp Stewart Co. purchased it and moved. With a name synonymous with quality and reliability, the new firm premises continued with output literally for the world, main railways, industrial sites all supplied with virtually every and any type of steam locomotive. Having produced 3,442 locos at the original Sharp Roberts' site, a continuation at the new works raised the total to 5,088 when a new beginning presented itself in 1903.

Still with worldwide markets and full order books, the three big locomotive works located in Glasgow decided to merge; Sharp Stewart Co. joined forces with Dubs & Co. and Neilson Reid. Thus was formed in 1903 the North British Locomotive Co. Ltd.

The three original works, Dubs & Co. at Queens Park, Neilson Reid at Hyde Park and Sharp Stewart at Atlas, retained their individual identification plates, and world production continued. Fifty years later, the end of steam was in sight, the last order for some of the largest locos of the lot were successfully completed, a dozen 4-8-2-2-8-4 Garretts on subcontract from Beyer Peacock. After the last loco was steamed in 1958, and a total of 26,755 steam locos from the records of three companies, North British Locomotive Co. Ltd, the largest locomotive firm in Europe, closed its doors and went into liquidation in 1962. The diesel had won!

R.B. Longridge & Co, Bedlington – 1785–1855

This interesting works, which received an order for six of Gooch's 2-2-2s in 1842, had one of the earliest starts of any of the general engineering works to obtain steam loco orders. The founder partnership of the Robert Stephenson Company had as a member Michael Longridge, who also ran his own company, the Bedlington Ironworks in the Blyth Valley in Northumberland. The general engineering output of the ironworks was such that it was a major employer in the early 1800s with about 1,500 workforce and a recognised apprenticeship facility.

Quality iron products included material for iron tyres for rolling stock, and, in line with its contemporaries, the firm commenced locomotive building in 1837, along with the rolling of iron rails and boiler plates for the Robert Stephenson concern.

Its first venture was one 0-6-0 for the Stanhope & Tyne Railway, commemorating by name, *Michael Longridge*, the works owner. Once into the locomotive business the Stephenson/Longridge partnership was destined to finish, which it did in 1842, and although they were building some long-boiler locos of the Stephenson format, these were probably orders separately obtained, not subcontracted by Stephenson.

In the two years following the construction of its first locomotive, the firm built about two dozen 2-2-2s for export to the expanding European market, so that when the Great Western order was received it was reasonably experienced in steam locomotive construction. Coincidentally (or maybe for old times' sake on ordering?) the father of the man who placed the orders, Gooch senior, had been employed at the Bedlington Works until about six years before locomotive construction started.

Order books remained full, both for export and home markets and orders for the 5ft gauge of the Eastern Counties Railways as well as for 4ft 8½in and the Great Western's broad gauge continued to come in. Ten 4-2-2s for the Bristol & Exeter 7ft, followed by a couple of 2-2-2 well tanks for the same company, covered 1849–51. Also in the latter year, five 4-4-0 saddle tanks were completed for the South Devon Railway, also in 7ft gauge.

Also at this time the firm completed an order of ten Crampton patent locos for the Great Western Railway, now the stamping ground of Archie Sturrock, whose early career had included association with Crampton when the latter had worked for about three years in the drawing office of the Great Western with Gooch. What could have been achieved if the two had remained with the Great Western?

The period 1851–52 was good and bad for the firm. Following the Cramptons came seven for the Midland Great Western Railway of Ireland (whose 5ft 3in gauge story is outlined elsewhere in this book), and then six for the Holyhead Breakwater Railway. The latter were to 7ft gauge, and were 0-4-0 well tanks with 3ft-diameter boilers, quite small really but designed for 110lbs per square inch pressure.

Quite suddenly it appears, there were no more orders forthcoming, and this production stopped. The company was sold in 1853, but presumably the purchaser could not make a go of it and the works finally shut down in 1855. Total output of steam locomotives had been about 200+ in the eighteen years of production, and the possibility that loco orders had taken over from the general engineering work on which the firm had established itself may have caused its downfall. It had been firmly established since 1785, and its concentration on steam locomotives may have whittled away its previous customers, all its eggs being in one basket!

Stothart, Slaughter & Co., Avon Street, Bristol – 1821–1888–1935

The opening of the railway age by the Stephensons in the 1820s triggered a spate of engineering firms opening for business building the steam locomotives, or expanding into the business from general engineering and stationary steam-engine building.

One of the former was Stothart & Co., which opened in 1837; when Edward Slaughter joined in 1841 its name was established. Whether as an industrial boost or because of favourable tendering quotes, Gooch made somewhat of a step into the unknown by giving the firm an order for two locomotives of the passenger batch of sixty-two 'Firefly' Class. The two were *Arrow* and *Dart* and must have been satisfactory as an order, for eight of the smaller 'Sun' Class followed, the usual 2-2-2 format but with smaller driving wheels.

The firm branched out in 1851 into shipbuilding, the locomotive works being known as the Avonside Ironworks, at this time also building for export as well as other British companies. The 7ft-gauge Birmingham & Gloucester Railway placed orders in the early 1840s for 2-2-2s, 0-6-0s and 2-4-0s, and the contract contained clauses giving the contractors control of the locomotive departments, and the supply of labour and stores for two years! Mr Stothart decided his future lay in shipbuilding interests, and his place was taken by Mr Gruning, thus giving the firm a change of name to Slaughter, Gruning & Co. in 1856.

Eight years later, after a succession of satisfactory orders from overseas, a pair of 0-8-0s was built for the Vale of Neath Railway, the patterns, stock and the goodwill of the name. The doors closed for the last time on 103 years of steam loco building, about 1,960 having rolled out of the works in that period, or about nineteen per year.

G. & J. Rennie – 1824–1890

This firm started in 1824 and had as one of its partner brothers a man whose name was to become famous in the civil engineering field – Sir John Rennie. The mechanical side of the business was handled by brother George, starting with the usual general engineering items and then, in keeping with many others of the period, jumping onto the rapidly growing bandwagon of steam loco manufacture in the 1830s.

The first order was for the London & Southampton Railway in 1838, and whilst the five of the order were completed and delivered, standards of construction were not as high as they should have been. The locos whilst still in almost new condition were almost totally rebuilt by W. Fairburn & Son during 1841. An order for a couple of 0-4-2s came from the London & Croydon Railway, and the designs included the same valve gear as the London & Southampton locos, that of Carmichael's patent, which used one fixed eccentric, not a particularly popular design.

A London & Brighton Railway order gave the firm more experience, and the export side was opened and just as rapidly closed with one order for Germany, which was not repeated! It was to this firm that Gooch gave his remaining order for two of his passenger batch, and possibly because of his detailed instructions and templates, the 7-footers were probably the best ever made by the firm. The Great Western pair named *Mazeppa* and *Arab* ran for almost thirty years, but most of the others rapidly gave problems.

G. & J. Rennie's locomotive-building efforts were not wholly successful and after struggling with the problem until about 1843 they gave up loco production and switched to marine steam engines, with which they had more success, finishing in the 1890s. In the five or so years of railway production and with the possible exception of Gooch's 7ft singles, a total of sixteen rather mediocre to poor locos had been rolled from the shops.

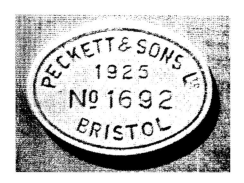

All companies had distinctive 'makers' plates'.

Summary

As soon as steam ceased to be considered the main motive power source for rail transport, irrespective of its still undeveloped potential, the writing was on the wall concerning the fate of the manufacturers. We have seen that some went out of business very early in the life of the steam locomotive, for reasons which were as relevant at the end of steam as at the beginning, when there was equally fierce competition. Many firms, in addition to those discussed, supplied steam locomotives to the Great Western and its constituent companies, and all of them ran into difficulties at some stage in their life due to failing or falling orders. Apart from failures, there were the inevitable mergers of famous names, which saw this measure as the only lifeline to stop them from being submerged.

Many firms diversified their business. We have seen the machine-tool makers that went into steam, and back into machine-tool making, and the firms that thrived on the export market and those that collapsed because of too much dependence on such outlets. Through all such problems, the workshops of the Great Western Railway still pressed through their own building and maintenance programmes, seemingly going from strength to strength, and dealing solely with the steam locomotives required for the Great Western.

With the reduction in the rail networks and abolition of steam from the system, it was inevitable that such a structure was doomed. It became a question of when, not if, the last of the works would close, as the whole concept of railway motive power had changed. Other sources were found for the new specialist manufacture, and, with the coming of the diesel ice age, the dinosaurs of steam and their environment became extinct.

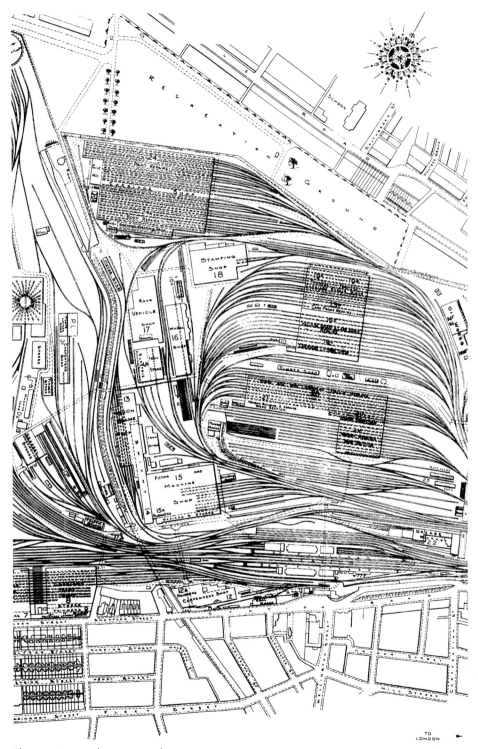

The carriage and wagon works.

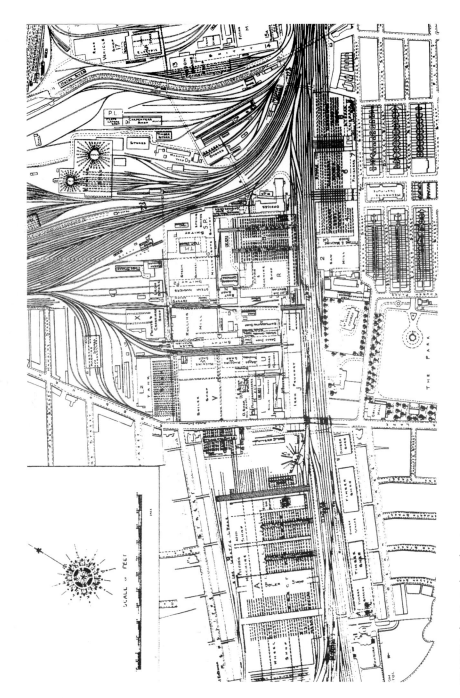

GWR Works, Swindon, the steam years.

If you enjoyed this book, you may also be interested in…

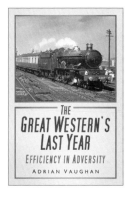

The Great Western's Last Year

ADRIAN VAUGHAN

Despite being one of the best-known and admired rail companies in the country, by 1947 the GWR was at the lowest ebb of its entire history. Worn out by war, there had been no maintenance for six years and the government couldn't supply the steel it needed for repair. The incredible strength of character and can-do attitude of GWR workers kept the railway running through it all. This history, taken from GWR papers and illustrated from them throughout, reveals how well they overcame their problems with only muscle power and a steam crane to help.

978 0 7524 6532 6

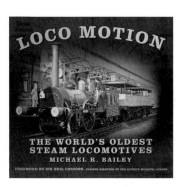

Loco Motion

MICHAEL BAILEY

The steam locomotive has inspired imagination, innovation and invention from the time of its origination. Here Michael R. Bailey describes the development of the steam locomotive during its pioneering first half-century by eexamining surviving locomotives and operable replicas, exploring their operational and preservation history, along with design characteristics, materials and modifications. With unparalleled detail, stunning images and a list of museums housing all of the world's oldest locomotives, this is an essential volume for all students of railway history

978 0 7524 9101 1

The Steam Locomotive Story

DAVID WRAGG

The steam locomotive was a British invention and even today, the world speed record for steam remains with a British locomotive, *Mallard*. Steam's first significant contribution to British industry was through powering pumping engines for mines. When steam was applied to the railways, the 'railway age' began. The steam locomotive went through several distinct phases during its long life, which came to an end on regular service in the late 1960s. This insightful, fully illustrated story book follows the history of the steam locomotive and will delight all those interested in the steam age.

978 0 7524 8806 6

Visit our website and discover thousands of other History Press books.

www.thehistorypress.co.uk